Mometrix
TEST PREPARATION

TExES

American Sign Language (ASL) (184) Secrets Study Guide

DEAR FUTURE EXAM SUCCESS STORY

First of all, **THANK YOU** for purchasing Mometrix study materials!

Second, congratulations! You are one of the few determined test-takers who are committed to doing whatever it takes to excel on your exam. **You have come to the right place.** We developed these study materials with one goal in mind: to deliver you the information you need in a format that's concise and easy to use.

In addition to optimizing your guide for the content of the test, we've outlined our recommended steps for breaking down the preparation process into small, attainable goals so you can make sure you stay on track.

We've also analyzed the entire test-taking process, identifying the most common pitfalls and showing how you can overcome them and be ready for any curveball the test throws you.

Standardized testing is one of the biggest obstacles on your road to success, which only increases the importance of doing well in the high-pressure, high-stakes environment of test day. Your results on this test could have a significant impact on your future, and this guide provides the information and practical advice to help you achieve your full potential on test day.

Your success is our success

We would love to hear from you! If you would like to share the story of your exam success or if you have any questions or comments in regard to our products, please contact us at **800-673-8175** or **support@mometrix.com**.

Thanks again for your business and we wish you continued success!

Sincerely,
The Mometrix Test Preparation Team

> **Need more help? Check out our flashcards at:**
> **http://mometrixflashcards.com/TExES**

TABLE OF CONTENTS

Introduction

Thank you for purchasing this resource! You have made the choice to prepare yourself for a test that could have a huge impact on your future, and this guide is designed to help you be fully ready for test day. Obviously, it's important to have a solid understanding of the test material, but you also need to be prepared for the unique environment and stressors of the test, so that you can perform to the best of your abilities.

For this purpose, the first section that appears in this guide is the **Secret Keys**. We've devoted countless hours to meticulously researching what works and what doesn't, and we've boiled down our findings to the five most impactful steps you can take to improve your performance on the test. We start at the beginning with study planning and move through the preparation process, all the way to the testing strategies that will help you get the most out of what you know when you're finally sitting in front of the test.

We recommend that you start preparing for your test as far in advance as possible. However, if you've bought this guide as a last-minute study resource and only have a few days before your test, we recommend that you skip over the first two Secret Keys since they address a long-term study plan.

If you struggle with **test anxiety**, we strongly encourage you to check out our recommendations for how you can overcome it. Test anxiety is a formidable foe, but it can be beaten, and we want to make sure you have the tools you need to defeat it.

1

Secret Key #1 – Plan Big, Study Small

There's a lot riding on your performance. If you want to ace this test, you're going to need to keep your skills sharp and the material fresh in your mind. You need a plan that lets you review everything you need to know while still fitting in your schedule. We'll break this strategy down into three categories.

Information Organization

Start with the information you already have: the official test outline. From this, you can make a complete list of all the concepts you need to cover before the test. Organize these concepts into groups that can be studied together, and create a list of any related vocabulary you need to learn so you can brush up on any difficult terms. You'll want to keep this vocabulary list handy once you actually start studying since you may need to add to it along the way.

Time Management

Once you have your set of study concepts, decide how to spread them out over the time you have left before the test. Break your study plan into small, clear goals so you have a manageable task for each day and know exactly what you're doing. Then just focus on one small step at a time. When you manage your time this way, you don't need to spend hours at a time studying. Studying a small block of content for a short period each day helps you retain information better and avoid stressing over how much you have left to do. You can relax knowing that you have a plan to cover everything in time. In order for this strategy to be effective though, you have to start studying early and stick to your schedule. Avoid the exhaustion and futility that comes from last-minute cramming!

Study Environment

The environment you study in has a big impact on your learning. Studying in a coffee shop, while probably more enjoyable, is not likely to be as fruitful as studying in a quiet room. It's important to keep distractions to a minimum. You're only planning to study for a short block of time, so make the most of it. Don't pause to check your phone or get up to find a snack. It's also important to **avoid multitasking**. Research has consistently shown that multitasking will make your studying dramatically less effective. Your study area should also be comfortable and well-lit so you don't have the distraction of straining your eyes or sitting on an uncomfortable chair.

 The time of day you study is also important. You want to be rested and alert. Don't wait until just before bedtime. Study when you'll be most likely to comprehend and remember. Even better, if you know what time of day your test will be, set that time aside for study. That way your brain will be used to working on that subject at that specific time and you'll have a better chance of recalling information.

Finally, it can be helpful to team up with others who are studying for the same test. Your actual studying should be done in as isolated an environment as possible, but the work of organizing the information and setting up the study plan can be divided up. In between study sessions, you can discuss with your teammates the concepts that you're all studying and quiz each other on the details. Just be sure that your teammates are as serious about the test as you are. If you find that your study time is being replaced with social time, you might need to find a new team.

2

Secret Key #2 – Make Your Studying Count

You're devoting a lot of time and effort to preparing for this test, so you want to be absolutely certain it will pay off. This means doing more than just reading the content and hoping you can remember it on test day. It's important to make every minute of study count. There are two main areas you can focus on to make your studying count.

Retention

It doesn't matter how much time you study if you can't remember the material. You need to make sure you are retaining the concepts. To check your retention of the information you're learning, try recalling it at later times with minimal prompting. Try carrying around flashcards and glance at one or two from time to time or ask a friend who's also studying for the test to quiz you.

To enhance your retention, look for ways to put the information into practice so that you can apply it rather than simply recalling it. If you're using the information in practical ways, it will be much easier to remember. Similarly, it helps to solidify a concept in your mind if you're not only reading it to yourself but also explaining it to someone else. Ask a friend to let you teach them about a concept you're a little shaky on (or speak aloud to an imaginary audience if necessary). As you try to summarize, define, give examples, and answer your friend's questions, you'll understand the concepts better and they will stay with you longer. Finally, step back for a big picture view and ask yourself how each piece of information fits with the whole subject. When you link the different concepts together and see them working together as a whole, it's easier to remember the individual components.

Finally, practice showing your work on any multi-step problems, even if you're just studying. Writing out each step you take to solve a problem will help solidify the process in your mind, and you'll be more likely to remember it during the test.

Modality

Modality simply refers to the means or method by which you study. Choosing a study modality that fits your own individual learning style is crucial. No two people learn best in exactly the same way, so it's important to know your strengths and use them to your advantage.

For example, if you learn best by visualization, focus on visualizing a concept in your mind and draw an image or a diagram. Try color-coding your notes, illustrating them, or creating symbols that will trigger your mind to recall a learned concept. If you learn best by hearing or discussing information, find a study partner who learns the same way or read aloud to yourself. Think about how to put the information in your own words. Imagine that you are giving a lecture on the topic and record yourself so you can listen to it later.

For any learning style, flashcards can be helpful. Organize the information so you can take advantage of spare moments to review. Underline key words or phrases. Use different colors for different categories. Mnemonic devices (such as creating a short list in which every item starts with the same letter) can also help with retention. Find what works best for you and use it to store the information in your mind most effectively and easily.

3

Secret Key #3 – Practice the Right Way

Your success on test day depends not only on how many hours you put into preparing, but also on whether you prepared the right way. It's good to check along the way to see if your studying is paying off. One of the most effective ways to do this is by taking practice tests to evaluate your progress. Practice tests are useful because they show exactly where you need to improve. Every time you take a practice test, pay special attention to these three groups of questions:

- The questions you got wrong
- The questions you had to guess on, even if you guessed right
- The questions you found difficult or slow to work through

This will show you exactly what your weak areas are, and where you need to devote more study time. Ask yourself why each of these questions gave you trouble. Was it because you didn't understand the material? Was it because you didn't remember the vocabulary? Do you need more repetitions on this type of question to build speed and confidence? Dig into those questions and figure out how you can strengthen your weak areas as you go back to review the material.

 Additionally, many practice tests have a section explaining the answer choices. It can be tempting to read the explanation and think that you now have a good understanding of the concept. However, an explanation likely only covers part of the question's broader context. Even if the explanation makes perfect sense, **go back and investigate** every concept related to the question until you're positive you have a thorough understanding.

As you go along, keep in mind that the practice test is just that: practice. Memorizing these questions and answers will not be very helpful on the actual test because it is unlikely to have any of the same exact questions. If you only know the right answers to the sample questions, you won't be prepared for the real thing. **Study the concepts** until you understand them fully, and then you'll be able to answer any question that shows up on the test.

It's important to wait on the practice tests until you're ready. If you take a test on your first day of study, you may be overwhelmed by the amount of material covered and how much you need to learn. Work up to it gradually.

On test day, you'll need to be prepared for answering questions, managing your time, and using the test-taking strategies you've learned. It's a lot to balance, like a mental marathon that will have a big impact on your future. Like training for a marathon, you'll need to start slowly and work your way up. When test day arrives, you'll be ready.

Start with the strategies you've read in the first two Secret Keys—plan your course and study in the way that works best for you. If you have time, consider using multiple study resources to get different approaches to the same concepts. It can be helpful to see difficult concepts from more than one angle. Then find a good source for practice tests. Many times, the test website will suggest potential study resources or provide sample tests.

Practice Test Strategy

If you're able to find at least three practice tests, we recommend this strategy:

UNTIMED AND OPEN-BOOK PRACTICE

Take the first test with no time constraints and with your notes and study guide handy. Take your time and focus on applying the strategies you've learned.

TIMED AND OPEN-BOOK PRACTICE

Take the second practice test open-book as well, but set a timer and practice pacing yourself to finish in time.

TIMED AND CLOSED-BOOK PRACTICE

Take any other practice tests as if it were test day. Set a timer and put away your study materials. Sit at a table or desk in a quiet room, imagine yourself at the testing center, and answer questions as quickly and accurately as possible.

Keep repeating timed and closed-book tests on a regular basis until you run out of practice tests or it's time for the actual test. Your mind will be ready for the schedule and stress of test day, and you'll be able to focus on recalling the material you've learned.

Secret Key #4 – Pace Yourself

Once you're fully prepared for the material on the test, your biggest challenge on test day will be managing your time. Just knowing that the clock is ticking can make you panic even if you have plenty of time left. Work on pacing yourself so you can build confidence against the time constraints of the exam. Pacing is a difficult skill to master, especially in a high-pressure environment, so **practice is vital**.

Set time expectations for your pace based on how much time is available. For example, if a section has 60 questions and the time limit is 30 minutes, you know you have to average 30 seconds or less per question in order to answer them all. Although 30 seconds is the hard limit, set 25 seconds per question as your goal, so you reserve extra time to spend on harder questions. When you budget extra time for the harder questions, you no longer have any reason to stress when those questions take longer to answer.

Don't let this time expectation distract you from working through the test at a calm, steady pace, but keep it in mind so you don't spend too much time on any one question. Recognize that taking extra time on one question you don't understand may keep you from answering two that you do understand later in the test. If your time limit for a question is up and you're still not sure of the answer, mark it and move on, and come back to it later if the time and the test format allow. If the testing format doesn't allow you to return to earlier questions, just make an educated guess; then put it out of your mind and move on.

On the easier questions, be careful not to rush. It may seem wise to hurry through them so you have more time for the challenging ones, but it's not worth missing one if you know the concept and just didn't take the time to read the question fully. Work efficiently but make sure you understand the question and have looked at all of the answer choices, since more than one may seem right at first.

Even if you're paying attention to the time, you may find yourself a little behind at some point. You should speed up to get back on track, but do so wisely. Don't panic; just take a few seconds less on each question until you're caught up. Don't guess without thinking, but do look through the answer choices and eliminate any you know are wrong. If you can get down to two choices, it is often worthwhile to guess from those. Once you've chosen an answer, move on and don't dwell on any that you skipped or had to hurry through. If a question was taking too long, chances are it was one of the harder ones, so you weren't as likely to get it right anyway.

On the other hand, if you find yourself getting ahead of schedule, it may be beneficial to slow down a little. The more quickly you work, the more likely you are to make a careless mistake that will affect your score. You've budgeted time for each question, so don't be afraid to spend that time. Practice an efficient but careful pace to get the most out of the time you have.

Secret Key #5 – Have a Plan for Guessing

When you're taking the test, you may find yourself stuck on a question. Some of the answer choices seem better than others, but you don't see the one answer choice that is obviously correct. What do you do?

The scenario described above is very common, yet most test takers have not effectively prepared for it. Developing and practicing a plan for guessing may be one of the single most effective uses of your time as you get ready for the exam.

In developing your plan for guessing, there are three questions to address:

- When should you start the guessing process?
- How should you narrow down the choices?
- Which answer should you choose?

When to Start the Guessing Process

Unless your plan for guessing is to select C every time (which, despite its merits, is not what we recommend), you need to leave yourself enough time to apply your answer elimination strategies. Since you have a limited amount of time for each question, that means that if you're going to give yourself the best shot at guessing correctly, you have to decide quickly whether or not you will guess.

Of course, the best-case scenario is that you don't have to guess at all, so first, see if you can answer the question based on your knowledge of the subject and basic reasoning skills. Focus on the key words in the question and try to jog your memory of related topics. Give yourself a chance to bring the knowledge to mind, but once you realize that you don't have (or you can't access) the knowledge you need to answer the question, it's time to start the guessing process.

It's almost always better to start the guessing process too early than too late. It only takes a few seconds to remember something and answer the question from knowledge. Carefully eliminating wrong answer choices takes longer. Plus, going through the process of eliminating answer choices can actually help jog your memory.

Summary: Start the guessing process as soon as you decide that you can't answer the question based on your knowledge.

How to Narrow Down the Choices

The next chapter in this book (**Test-Taking Strategies**) includes a wide range of strategies for how to approach questions and how to look for answer choices to eliminate. You will definitely want to read those carefully, practice them, and figure out which ones work best for you. Here though, we're going to address a mindset rather than a particular strategy.

Your odds of guessing an answer correctly depend on how many options you are choosing from.

Number of options left	5	4	3	2	1
Odds of guessing correctly	20%	25%	33%	50%	100%

You can see from this chart just how valuable it is to be able to eliminate incorrect answers and make an educated guess, but there are two things that many test takers do that cause them to miss out on the benefits of guessing:

- Accidentally eliminating the correct answer
- Selecting an answer based on an impression

We'll look at the first one here, and the second one in the next section.

To avoid accidentally eliminating the correct answer, we recommend a thought exercise called **the $5 challenge**. In this challenge, you only eliminate an answer choice from contention if you are willing to bet $5 on it being wrong. Why $5? Five dollars is a small but not insignificant amount of money. It's an amount you could afford to lose but wouldn't want to throw away. And while losing

$5 once might not hurt too much, doing it twenty times will set you back $100. In the same way, each small decision you make—eliminating a choice here, guessing on a question there—won't by itself impact your score very much, but when you put them all together, they can make a big difference. By holding each answer choice elimination decision to a higher standard, you can reduce the risk of accidentally eliminating the correct answer.

The $5 challenge can also be applied in a positive sense: If you are willing to bet $5 that an answer choice *is* correct, go ahead and mark it as correct.

Summary: Only eliminate an answer choice if you are willing to bet $5 that it is wrong.

8

Which Answer to Choose

You're taking the test. You've run into a hard question and decided you'll have to guess. You've eliminated all the answer choices you're willing to bet $5 on. Now you have to pick an answer. Why do we even need to talk about this? Why can't you just pick whichever one you feel like when the time comes?

The answer to these questions is that if you don't come into the test with a plan, you'll rely on your impression to select an answer choice, and if you do that, you risk falling into a trap. The test writers know that everyone who takes their test will be guessing on some of the questions, so they intentionally write wrong answer choices to seem plausible. You still have to pick an answer though, and if the wrong answer choices are designed to look right, how can you ever be sure that you're not falling for their trap? The best solution we've found to this dilemma is to take the decision out of your hands entirely. Here is the process we recommend:

Once you've eliminated any choices that you are confident (willing to bet $5) are wrong, select the first remaining choice as your answer.

Whether you choose to select the first remaining choice, the second, or the last, the important thing is that you use some preselected standard. Using this approach guarantees that you will not be enticed into selecting an answer choice that looks right, because you are not basing your decision on how the answer choices look.

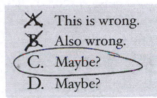

This is not meant to make you question your knowledge. Instead, it is to help you recognize the difference between your knowledge and your impressions. There's a huge difference between thinking an answer is right because of what you know, and thinking an answer is right because it looks or sounds like it should be right.

Summary: To ensure that your selection is appropriately random, make a predetermined selection from among all answer choices you have not eliminated.

Test-Taking Strategies

This section contains a list of test-taking strategies that you may find helpful as you work through the test. By taking what you know and applying logical thought, you can maximize your chances of answering any question correctly!

It is very important to realize that every question is different and every person is different: no single strategy will work on every question, and no single strategy will work for every person. That's why we've included all of them here, so you can try them out and determine which ones work best for different types of questions and which ones work best for you.

Question Strategies

☑ READ CAREFULLY

Read the question and the answer choices carefully. Don't miss the question because you misread the terms. You have plenty of time to read each question thoroughly and make sure you understand what is being asked. Yet a happy medium must be attained, so don't waste too much time. You must read carefully and efficiently.

☑ CONTEXTUAL CLUES

Look for contextual clues. If the question includes a word you are not familiar with, look at the immediate context for some indication of what the word might mean. Contextual clues can often give you all the information you need to decipher the meaning of an unfamiliar word. Even if you can't determine the meaning, you may be able to narrow down the possibilities enough to make a solid guess at the answer to the question.

☑ PREFIXES

If you're having trouble with a word in the question or answer choices, try dissecting it. Take advantage of every clue that the word might include. Prefixes can be a huge help. Usually, they allow you to determine a basic meaning. *Pre-* means before, *post-* means after, *pro-* is positive, *de-* is negative. From prefixes, you can get an idea of the general meaning of the word and try to put it into context.

☑ HEDGE WORDS

Watch out for critical hedge words, such as *likely, may, can, sometimes, often, almost, mostly, usually, generally, rarely,* and *sometimes*. Question writers insert these hedge phrases to cover every possibility. Often an answer choice will be wrong simply because it leaves no room for exception. Be on guard for answer choices that have definitive words such as *exactly* and *always*.

☑ SWITCHBACK WORDS

Stay alert for *switchbacks*. These are the words and phrases frequently used to alert you to shifts in thought. The most common switchback words are *but, although,* and *however*. Others include *nevertheless, on the other hand, even though, while, in spite of, despite,* and *regardless of*. Switchback words are important to catch because they can change the direction of the question or an answer choice.

⊘ FACE VALUE

When in doubt, use common sense. Accept the situation in the problem at face value. Don't read too much into it. These problems will not require you to make wild assumptions. If you have to go beyond creativity and warp time or space in order to have an answer choice fit the question, then you should move on and consider the other answer choices. These are normal problems rooted in reality. The applicable relationship or explanation may not be readily apparent, but it is there for you to figure out. Use your common sense to interpret anything that isn't clear.

Answer Choice Strategies

⊘ ANSWER SELECTION

The most thorough way to pick an answer choice is to identify and eliminate wrong answers until only one is left, then confirm it is the correct answer. Sometimes an answer choice may immediately seem right, but be careful. The test writers will usually put more than one reasonable answer choice on each question, so take a second to read all of them and make sure that the other choices are not equally obvious. As long as you have time left, it is better to read every answer choice than to pick the first one that looks right without checking the others.

⊘ ANSWER CHOICE FAMILIES

An answer choice family consists of two (in rare cases, three) answer choices that are very similar in construction and cannot all be true at the same time. If you see two answer choices that are direct opposites or parallels, one of them is usually the correct answer. For instance, if one answer choice says that quantity x increases and another either says that quantity x decreases (opposite) or says that quantity y increases (parallel), then those answer choices would fall into the same family. An answer choice that doesn't match the construction of the answer choice family is more likely to be incorrect. Most questions will not have answer choice families, but when they do appear, you should be prepared to recognize them.

⊘ ELIMINATE ANSWERS

Eliminate answer choices as soon as you realize they are wrong, but make sure you consider all possibilities. If you are eliminating answer choices and realize that the last one you are left with is also wrong, don't panic. Start over and consider each choice again. There may be something you missed the first time that you will realize on the second pass.

⊘ AVOID FACT TRAPS

Don't be distracted by an answer choice that is factually true but doesn't answer the question. You are looking for the choice that answers the question. Stay focused on what the question is asking for so you don't accidentally pick an answer that is true but incorrect. Always go back to the question and make sure the answer choice you've selected actually answers the question and is not merely a true statement.

⊘ EXTREME STATEMENTS

In general, you should avoid answers that put forth extreme actions as standard practice or proclaim controversial ideas as established fact. An answer choice that states the "process should be used in certain situations, if..." is much more likely to be correct than one that states the "process should be discontinued completely." The first is a calm rational statement and doesn't even make a definitive, uncompromising stance, using a hedge word *if* to provide wiggle room, whereas the second choice is far more extreme.

⊘ Benchmark

As you read through the answer choices and you come across one that seems to answer the question well, mentally select that answer choice. This is not your final answer, but it's the one that will help you evaluate the other answer choices. The one that you selected is your benchmark or standard for judging each of the other answer choices. Every other answer choice must be compared to your benchmark. That choice is correct until proven otherwise by another answer choice beating it. If you find a better answer, then that one becomes your new benchmark. Once you've decided that no other choice answers the question as well as your benchmark, you have your final answer.

⊘ Predict the Answer

Before you even start looking at the answer choices, it is often best to try to predict the answer. When you come up with the answer on your own, it is easier to avoid distractions and traps because you will know exactly what to look for. The right answer choice is unlikely to be word-for-word what you came up with, but it should be a close match. Even if you are confident that you have the right answer, you should still take the time to read each option before moving on.

General Strategies

⊘ Tough Questions

If you are stumped on a problem or it appears too hard or too difficult, don't waste time. Move on! Remember though, if you can quickly check for obviously incorrect answer choices, your chances of guessing correctly are greatly improved. Before you completely give up, at least try to knock out a couple of possible answers. Eliminate what you can and then guess at the remaining answer choices before moving on.

⊘ Check Your Work

Since you will probably not know every term listed and the answer to every question, it is important that you get credit for the ones that you do know. Don't miss any questions through careless mistakes. If at all possible, try to take a second to look back over your answer selection and make sure you've selected the correct answer choice and haven't made a costly careless mistake (such as marking an answer choice that you didn't mean to mark). This quick double check should more than pay for itself in caught mistakes for the time it costs.

⊘ Pace Yourself

It's easy to be overwhelmed when you're looking at a page full of questions; your mind is confused and full of random thoughts, and the clock is ticking down faster than you would like. Calm down and maintain the pace that you have set for yourself. Especially as you get down to the last few minutes of the test, don't let the small numbers on the clock make you panic. As long as you are on track by monitoring your pace, you are guaranteed to have time for each question.

⊘ Don't Rush

It is very easy to make errors when you are in a hurry. Maintaining a fast pace in answering questions is pointless if it makes you miss questions that you would have gotten right otherwise. Test writers like to include distracting information and wrong answers that seem right. Taking a little extra time to avoid careless mistakes can make all the difference in your test score. Find a pace that allows you to be confident in the answers that you select.

12

⊘ Keep Moving

Panicking will not help you pass the test, so do your best to stay calm and keep moving. Taking deep breaths and going through the answer elimination steps you practiced can help to break through a stress barrier and keep your pace.

Final Notes

The combination of a solid foundation of content knowledge and the confidence that comes from practicing your plan for applying that knowledge is the key to maximizing your performance on test day. As your foundation of content knowledge is built up and strengthened, you'll find that the strategies included in this chapter become more and more effective in helping you quickly sift through the distractions and traps of the test to isolate the correct answer.

Now that you're preparing to move forward into the test content chapters of this book, be sure to keep your goal in mind. As you read, think about how you will be able to apply this information on the test. If you've already seen sample questions for the test and you have an idea of the question format and style, try to come up with questions of your own that you can answer based on what you're reading. This will give you valuable practice applying your knowledge in the same ways you can expect to on test day.

Good luck and good studying!

General Language Acquisition

LANGUAGE ACQUISITION

Children acquire language gradually throughout their first few years in five basic stages. Newborns distinguish among speech sounds within two months of birth and most infants understand some words between four and nine months. At around six months, cooing appears, even in congenitally deaf infants. Phonemes from every language are uttered during this stage. At six to eight months, infants babble. The holophrastic stage of one-word utterances is from nine to eighteen months. Syntax, or combining words, appears in the second year. Multi-word utterances may leave out grammatical morphemes; these are called telegraphic speech. In the next year, sentences become longer, grammatical elements are more often correctly used and sentences with multiple clauses become more common. At five to six years of age, children have developed almost normal speech. Deaf children progress through similar stages and studies show they learn sign language at roughly the same rate that hearing children learn to speak.

DEVELOPMENTAL SPEECH AND LANGUAGE MILESTONES

FIRST YEAR OF LIFE

Children go through many developmental milestones in speech and language in their first year of life. In the first three months of life, babies learn to recognize and respond to familiar voices and smiles when their mother comes into view. The baby repeats sounds and uses a different cry for different situations. Between four and six months, infants recognize changes in tone of voice as well as sounds other than speech. At this age, babies respond to the word "no", engage in vocal play, and can make urgent noises to prompt a response from a caregiver. Seven- to twelve-month-old infants turn to look when their name is called, recognize the names of familiar objects, and begin to respond to questions or requests. At this stage, they also use more consonants in babbling and make sounds other than crying. This is when the child's first words appear.

YEARS ONE THROUGH FOUR

A child's speech development expands along with their vocabulary after their first year. At one- to two-years-old the child follows simple commands, can name some body parts and point to named pictures in a book. One-year-olds enjoy repetition as well as rhymes, simple songs and stories. The child at this age makes stage-1 sentences (morphemes average 1.75) and can ask two-word questions. Spoken words become clearer. He enjoys songs, rhymes and simple stories. At two to three years, two-stage commands are understood as well as differences like hot and cold. Vocabulary grows fast. Questions that ask 'what' or 'where' are understood by the three- to four-year-old. Children at this age use sentences of four more words. They can talk about things that happened away from home. At four to five years, children speak clearly, constructing detailed sentences and answering simple questions about stories. "R", "th" and "v" sounds may still be difficult to pronounce.

SIGN LANGUAGE USAGE BY PEOPLE WHO ARE NOT DEAF

Sign language is often used as a means of communication with children who have speech delay or impairment. Sign language is also used extensively with children with autism to give them a means of communication when verbal communication is difficult. Using sign language provides social and behavioral benefits. Social interaction improves and behavioral difficulties are reduced when children have a way to express themselves. Signed English is usually taught rather than ASL because it uses the same grammar and word order as spoken English. This use of sign language is a form of Augmentative and Alternative Communication (AAC). Another use of sign language by hearing children is the popular baby sign program. Children can communicate using signs before they learn to use speech and evidence shows that learning sign language increases the rate at which spoken language is learned.

NOAM CHOMSKY THEORY

According to Chomsky, language acquisition is innate and all humans acquire language, unless a physical or mental limitation is present. He believed that because children use linguistic structures so accurately, independent of external experience, the structures must be already imprinted on the mind. Chomsky proposed that a 'language acquisition device' or LAD is the part of the brain that processes language and whether or not combinations of words make sense to a person is something individuals comprehend spontaneously. Chomsky's generative theory proposed that all grammar is explained by a single set of rules. Chomsky's theory of generative grammar has been called the most important contribution in the field of theoretical linguistics in the twentieth century.

BICS AND CALP

Basic Interpersonal Communication Skills, or BICS, is everyday language such as that which is used socially. Conversations on the playground, on the telephone or in the lunchroom employ these language skills. BICS does not require the use of specialized language or a high degree of cognition as it uses known ideas and vocabulary. This level of skill usually develops in six to twenty-four months when learning a second language.

Cognitive Academic Language Proficiency, or CALP, is needed for success in academic learning. CALP involves skills such as classifying, evaluating, comparing, and inferring. When this level is achieved, the student is able to plan, take notes and ask questions. Learners use cognitive, metacognitive and social-affective strategies to learn cooperatively and to self-reflect. Development of Cognitive Academic Language Proficiency takes five years or more.

FUNCTIONS OF LANGUAGE

The functional-notional approach to language learning categorizes five functions of language. Functions are communicative acts wherein language is used for a specific purpose. Learning useful expressions gives even beginning students ways to communicate purposefully.

Personal language - expresses thoughts or feelings in the physical and emotional realms, such as hunger or happiness

Interpersonal language - used in social and working relationships to make introductions or appointments, express agreement or disagreement, to interrupt or change the subject

Directive language - accepts or refuses direction, makes requests or suggestions, tries to persuade, or gives direction

Referential language - talks about people, things, actions, or events in the past or future; it defines, explains or compares, evaluates or requests. It is the metalinguistic function.

Imaginative language – involves elements of creative expression; can be applied to discussions of poetry or artwork and problem solving

EYE CONTACT

As early as the first month, infants develop eye contact behavior. Dyadic eye contact, a relatively simple mechanism that determines whether a person's gaze is averted or directed, helps infants develop and regulate both verbal and nonverbal social interaction. Triadic eye gaze involves a third

16

person or object. From observing a person's focus of attention, internal states, such as desire, can be inferred. Triadic eye gaze is critical in human interaction. Its beginning development is seen at around six months and is thought to be necessary for acquiring language. Eye contact may signal interest, difficulty in understanding, or be used to facilitate turn taking. Watching others' faces, especially their eyes, may reinforce certain behaviors and stimulate responses or extinguish them. Failure to develop eye contact is noted in children with autism. An important developmental milestone is met when children learn to divide their attention between people and objects.

PIAGET VS. VYGOTSKY

According to Vygotsky, cognitive development is the result of interaction between the child's abilities and his social experiences He proposed the social dimension of consciousness as primary, while the individual dimension is derivative. Piaget argued that the child learns about relationships between people and objects through his experiences manipulating the world. Piaget thought that children's learning was predictable, following certain stages. Vygotsky held that each child had an individual sequence dependent on his specific social environment and unique cultural experiences. For Vygotsky, higher order cognitive functions begin in social interactions. For Piaget, learning depends on development, which he regarded as internal, while learning was an external process. Vygotsky saw learning and development as interdependent, the relationship of which is explained by his Zone of Proximal Development (ZPD). In the ZPD, concepts and principles can be successfully applied to new tasks; thus learning occurs.

FIRST AND SECOND LANGUAGE ACQUISITION

Infants learning their first language have not only highly malleable brains, but they are not yet distracted by other commitments and distractions. Ordinarily infants are supplied intense support from caregivers. Almost every child will achieve mastery of their native language. Language learning in children is related to their needs and interests. It is not arranged in sequence; language used adapts to the situation and is extended through play. Second language learners are already familiar with human society and the world. Their learning is affected by attitudes, personality and motivation. Their brains are engaged in multiple tasks. Fossilization may occur and mastery of the language isn't a given. Both first and second language learners are discovering meaning of words; patterns of sentence construction; striving for fluency; and both benefit from a rich language environment.

TURN TAKING VS. CONSTRUCTED DIALOG

Nonmanual signals play a part in turn taking. Eye gaze is an important element in conversations. The custom in sign language conversations is for one person to sign at a time and to indicate when he is finished. A signer may begin signing when there is a pause in the conversation. When someone interrupts a signer, the signer may refuse to give up his turn, indicating this by lowering or averting his eyes, holding up an index finger or an open hand. Some situations have formal rules: in the classroom, the teacher often selects; in a courtroom, attorneys typically ask the questions. In regular conversation, the signer self-selects or takes his turn when asked a question.

A constructed dialog reports a conversation that has already taken place. The reported dialog can take place between hypothetical persons or be anthropomorphic. The signer shifts her body and eye gaze to indicate when another person is talking. The speech is not necessarily verbatim.

TURN TAKING IN AND OUT OF THE CLASSROOM

In the classroom, attention is centralized, often on the instructor. Lessons are preplanned and turns are allocated with less opportunity for negotiation than in natural discourse. Teachers maintain the right to speak and interrupt. When the teacher participates as facilitator instead of knower, more natural turn taking can take place.

Natural conversation has cultural rules for politeness. Some cultures expect and permit interruptions or simultaneous speaking whereas other cultures expect a speaker to wait a few seconds before an utterance.

Infants learn turn taking according to culture as well. In the West, caregivers respond to baby noises, even burps or sneezes. These interactions help form routines of turn taking; patterns are usually established in the first year.

SIGNALING CONVERSATIONAL TURN TAKING

Turn taking in conversation is highly organized. The rules work not only to avoid gaps but also to prevent overlap in conversation. Most interactions permit one speaker at a time. Transition to another speaker is often made when the person speaking selects another speaker. Gesture or eye gaze are ways of indicating this choice. Other indicators are imbedded in the speech; it may become softer, a last syllable drawn out, or words used that suggest the speech is finished. Rising or falling tone are implicit markers, as is body language. Explicit markers include making a suggestion, request, or asking a question. Rules for getting and giving up the floor may be subtle. A pause is the most common signal. Strategies for keeping the floor include running sentences together with connecters, such as like, so, but, etc. Pausing where the message is incomplete also keeps control of the turn.

PRIVATE VS. SELF-DIRECTED SPEECH

Although they didn't agree on its role, both Piaget and Vygotsky were interested in private speech in children. Private speech continues throughout one's life, but is more frequently used in childhood. Private speech is a way second language learners regulate their utterances. When language learners lack mastery, they use private speech to try out their responses. It allows manipulation of language and hypothesis testing covertly and is thought to be an intermediary between social and inner speech. Whether spoken out loud or not, it is a means of internalizing the L2. Private speech does not adapt to an audience; it is produced only for the self. Occasions for private speech result incidentally; hearing others speak triggers mental activity.

ENCOURAGING LANGUAGE AND SPEECH DEVELOPMENT

With pre-verbal infants, the parent or teacher engages in proto-conversations - when the child responds to speech with cooing, smiling, eye contact or mouth movements, the adult continues the conversation as though the child had taken his or her turn. Language modeling using simple words and basic sentences includes talking to the child, as well as narrating what is going on around him, giving words for objects and actions. Expanding on the child's vocalization, such as adding adjectives, promotes imitation and understanding. Playtime is an optimum time to model conversational practices, to make comments and explain things. Singing simple, familiar songs is another way to make language fun and interesting for a child. Offering choices gives the child an opportunity to respond with a word or gesture. Language that occurs naturally during ordinary situations is a fundamental strategy. Praise for communicative effort, as well as an unhurried manner keeps language learning from becoming stressful.

SALK INSTITUTE

At the Laboratory for Cognitive Neuroscience at the Salk Institute for Biological Studies in San Diego, California, researchers under the direction of Ursula Bellugi study how ASL is processed in the brain. They hope to discover which neural regions are engaged in processing linguistic facial expressions and other elements of language. Studying signed languages helps reveal the relation between cognition and language and may prove which aspects of language processing are universal. Using eye-tracking technology, researchers are trying to prove the theory that eye gaze is a grammatical function in ASL. Bellugi's work helped show ASL to be a true language.

ASL SIGNS ARE ELEMENTS OF LANGUAGE

A common misconception is that ASL represents spoken English through hand gestures. American Sign Language is not just a series of gestures or mime. Signs are constrained by a finite set of handshapes and movements as well as the deliberate use of space. Gestures do not have standard forms; they are created at the moment of speaking and are not controlled by linguistic structure. A basic principle of language is that smaller parts combine into larger wholes. The features of ASL combine to form signs and sentences. Units of language are consistently produced in a way that is recognized by the language community.

FULLY ARTICULATED SOCIOLINGUISTIC VARIATIONS

There are unique differences in social constraints applied to Deaf communities. Ethnicity, regional background, age, and gender will be defined differently. For example, differences in signing may be attributed to age or to changes in educational policy. Regional background may not be as significant a constraint as where a person went to school. Minority Deaf communities may also account for language differences; as well as economic factors as they intersect with race, gender, and political groups. Language may be acquired from native-speaking parents or much later in life. Exposure to other kinds of signing, such as Signed English, will also have an effect on language development. There is also a difficulty in observing and recording natural signed conversation.

WILLIAM STOKOE

The idea that it was possible to analyze signed language was not welcomed at first. Many other Gallaudet faculty members didn't hold respect for signing; some were afraid it would undermine their teaching practices; others may have been jealous. Many people had internalized a negative view of sign language; oralism was the dominant educational philosophy. Stokoe's work challenged it as the best way to teach the deaf. The work was treated with indifference at best. The complex names and strange words Stokoe came up with to designate handshapes and movements, as well as the transcription system he devised, were difficult to learn and understand. The deaf were offended that a hearing person who didn't know how sign very well would undertake the task of analyzing it.

Stokoe identified three parts of signs that are combined simultaneously: the location, or tabula (tab); the handshape or designator (dez); and the movement or signation (sig). Stokoe called the parameters cheremes, from the Greek word for hand and defined them as "meaningless elements that combine to form signs just as phonemes combine to form words." He developed symbols for each tab, dez and sig.

By studying movement of parts of the body, points of contact, speed, and repetition Stokoe recognized the elements of signs. He identified prime members for each parameter: A, B, and 5 for handshapes; face, nose, and trunk for locations; and upward, downward, and away from the signer as prime movements. Before Stokoe's system of analysis, signs were regarded as wholes.

Stokoe was driven not only to understand sign language, but also desired to treat the deaf with dignity. Working at the Language Research Lab in his spare time, Stokoe collaborated with deaf researchers, whom he treated as equals. His study led to the designation American Sign Language, increasing interest and respect for what had been known as the Signed Language. His work created deaf sign linguistics, a new branch of research. Although Chomsky had made linguistics popular, sign language had so far not been considered as a language. Following Trager, Stokoe thought of language as part of culture. He could see that morphemes are not structured mechanically. Though it took ten years after his Dictionary of American Sign Language (DASL) was published, classes in the structure of ASL began to be taught at Gallaudet. His work brought recognition of deaf culture.

BOSTON UNIVERSITY SCHOOL OF EDUCATION CENTER FOR THE STUDY OF COMMUNICATION

The Center for the Study of Communication and the Deaf conducts applied and theoretical research in three major areas: the acquisition of signed languages, how language impacts the education of Deaf children, and developmental assessment of bilingual approaches to Deaf education. One project is focused on the relationship between ASL and learning to read. In September 2010, a grant was obtained from the US Department of Education to develop an instrument to assess knowledge of ASL in Deaf children. The American Signed Language Assessment Instrument (ASLAI) measures academic and conversational language ability, the first validated educational assessment of American Sign Language. The tool will identify children who have learning disabilities or need language intervention.

HINDRANCES TO THE RESEARCH

Most deaf children are born to hearing parents, so relatively few sign language users are indigenous members of the language community. Interaction among deaf and hearing people is not well documented and assumptions have been made about the deaf community that fail to take into consideration its diversity and complexity. The process whereby sign languages mature is not fully understood; the origins of many ASL signs have been handed down as folklore. The predominance of the oral method of teaching leaves a gap in ASL history.

Archives from deaf schools and narratives have helped trace the history of deaf culture and sign language. Films were made in the early 1900's that document a register of ASL no longer in use - the classic register of oratory. Comparison of different genres, such as lecture or storytelling, and knowledge of language contact has helped researchers to understand some of the similarities and differences in signed languages.

MANUALLY CODED ENGLISH (MCE)

A number of codes have been invented to represent English manually. The signs are accompanied by the spoken or mouthed English word.

Seeing Essential English (SEE1) was developed by David Anthony, a deaf educator at the Michigan School for the Deaf. SEE1 uses a movement for each syllable.

Signing Exact English (SEE2) uses some ASL signs and many invented initialized signs. Each sign translates to one English word.

Signed English (SE) uses ASL and initialized signs in English grammatical order. It uses simultaneous speech and is used as an educational tool. SE uses sign markers and fingerspelling.

Conceptually Accurate Signed English (CASE) blends American Sign Language (ASL) and Manually Coded English (MCE), taking into account meaning, rather than word for word translation, and fingerspelling for words that don't have a sign.

The Rochester method, used for a time at the Rochester School for the Deaf, is based on English and fingerspells each word.

SIGN LANGUAGE UNDERSTOOD UNIVERSALLY

Many countries have their own sign languages — from the Auslan of Australia to the Zimsign of Zimbabwe – some of which are recognized constitutionally. The sign language used in the United States, ASL, is also used in the areas of Canada where English is spoken. The French areas use LSF, Langue des Signes Française, the precursor to ASL. British Sign Language, BSL, developed separately from ASL and is very different. The British manual alphabet uses both hands; signs for ASL letters are made with only one hand.

There is no universal sign language used and understood worldwide. An International Sign Language, IS, formerly known as Gestuno, was developed by the World Federation of the Deaf. It is, like Esperanto, a constructed language. Chosen from among national signs as the most easily understood, IS is a vocabulary of signs agreed upon for use at international meetings.

ASL LEXICON

It is estimated that as much as 60% of the ASL lexicon derives from early French Sign Language (LSF). Both LSF and ASL have a number of sources including gestures and home signs used by deaf individuals among hearing families. ASL is influenced by North American Indian sign languages and Martha's Vineyard sign language, with new signs having been added through the generations. Cistercian Sign Language (CSL), used by monks, has many signs similar to early LSL. As in spoken languages, signs are borrowed from other countries, for example, pizza is a borrowed word. New terms are coined as technology advances; cultural change and social interaction add to the lexicon of ASL as well, just as it does in spoken languages.

FEATURES OF OTHER COMMUNICATION SYSTEMS

Language shows relationship between symbols. New symbols are constantly added to languages and can be broken down into smaller parts and have different functions. Language can be used to express any topic and can express past, future and conditional tenses. Language changes over time through interaction. All users can send and receive messages, as well as self-correct. Language is learned from other users.

In other communication systems, like Morse code, symbols occur in sequence, from which meaning is derived. The set of symbols used is finite; with each symbol a constant and discrete unit with one meaning. Symbols express the immediate and present and do not change across time through natural use. Communication by a system of symbols is limited to survival or emergency management.

PANTOMIME VS. ASL

Pantomimes vary from person to person. An ASL sign is recognized from person to person because it uses a particular standardized handshape. Pantomimes include a number of actions and are longer in duration. ASL signs use one action and are short in duration. In pantomime, the hands go through preparatory motions. In signing, hands begin in a resting position with no specific shape and the handshape is briefly held in position. The pantomime is freer, not limited to the conventional handshapes for ASL. The hands move differently and independently, unlike ASL. Pantomimes do not hold to the conventions of signing space for ASL. The eyes follow the hands, unlike in ASL where direct eye contact is the norm.

PRIMARY AND ALTERNATE SIGNED LANGUAGES

A primary sign language is the first, or only, language of a deaf population. Language grows from social intercourse; it cannot be invented. Real languages contain the wisdom and knowledge of those who share and have shared a culture. Primary sign languages are visual and spatial because vision is the channel, the only channel deaf can effectively use.

Alternate sign languages are used when speech is prohibited for some reason, such as among the monks who made vows of silence. Australian aboriginal tribes use an alternate sign language for ritual reasons. Among the Plains Indians, sign was the lingua franca among tribes. Alternate sign languages do not evolve through social needs. Boy Scout signs are another example of an alternate sign language. Manual codes serve a number of purposes, but they do not reflect the culture and knowledge of the speech group; they are not adopted by the Deaf as a primary language.

AL-SAYYID BEDOUIN SIGN LANGUAGE VS. JORDANIAN SIGN LANGUAGE

Al-Sayyid Bedouin Sign Language (ABSL) is relatively young; a new sign language not based on any spoken language. It is evolving from apparent homesign to a fully formed language. ABSL is in its third generation; members of the community who are deaf (about 150 persons) are descended from two brothers. Changes can be observed in each generation and traced easily due to the stable social network of the community.

Jordanian Sign Language (Lughat al-Ishara al-Urdunia, LIU) seems to be related to other Middle Eastern sign languages and has a number of dialects. Only half of Jordan's deaf children receive education, as such, LIU does not use extensive fingerspelling or initialized sings. In LIU, spatial relationships are not commonly established in storytelling. Mouthing in LIU derives from the vernacular and common gestures have been integrated into the language.

CHINESE SIGN LANGUAGE (CSL) VS. AMERICAN SIGN LANGUAGE (ASL)

What appear to be virtually the same sign in Chinese Sign Language (CSL) and American Sign Language (ASL) are two different lexical items. For example, the sign in ASL which means "secret," is the sign for "father" in CSL. Some Chinese signs are made with a combination of forms that are possible in ASL, but are not ASL signs. Some Chinese signs use formations that are not possible in ASL because they use points of contact or handshapes not found in ASL. As spoken languages have subtle differences, so ASL and CSL also exhibit slight differences. The closed fist handshape in ASL is less rigid than the corresponding handshape in CSL in which the thumb is extended and the fingers overlap more of the palm; a pinching handshape is used in different combinations across the two languages. Prime handshapes are consistent within each language but not across the languages.

AMERICAN INDIAN NATIONS OF THE GREAT PLAINS

The Plains Sign Language is an artificial sign language developed to make communication possible between the many different Indian nations which each spoke many different languages. Among the tribes, no one language was dominant. Origins of the language are unknown, but sixteenth century explorers made note of the Indians using signs. It was used because of the nomadic lifestyle, to facilitate trading, for making alliances, and for social reasons. Many Plains signs are iconic and therefore easier to learn than arbitrary signals. Signing was also used within tribes; differences in dialect did not prohibit communication between these tribes. Signs or gestures did not carry the stigma of being lower than spoken language. Plains Sign Language, as well as native spoken languages of the tribes, has gradually been replaced, though signing is still used ceremonially and in storytelling.

FOREIGNNESS

While textbooks suggest that presenting positive images of the target culture is a way to overcome negative stereotypes, it is necessary to actively combat them. Conceptualization of one's own or another culture is not readily relinquished; that customs, values and expectations are participated in subconsciously needs to be explored. Comparison of the target culture with the native language speaker's can help identify common ground. Emphasis on cultural experience rather than cultural awareness will help minimize the "otherness" of the culture being explored, as well. Songs and stories in both languages should be enjoyed. Realia in the classroom helps students to construct a mental image.

SAPIR-WHORF HYPOTHESIS

The Sapir-Whorf hypothesis proposes linguistic relativity: languages that are of the same family—Indo-European, for example—produce similarities in experience and thought and that languages that are especially disparate lead to more pronounced differences in worldview. The hypothesis makes two claims: that languages differ from one another in important ways; and that the language one uses influences his conceptualization of the world. Linguistic relativity was discussed in the late 1700's in Germany. American anthropologist Sapir, writing in 1929, said that the 'real world' is largely built on the language habits of the group. Whorf, who was Sapir's student, stated even more boldly that our thoughts are "at the mercy" of our language; this view is known as linguistic determinism.

SOCIOCULTURAL THEORY AND CONSTRUCTIVIST THEORY

Sociocultural theory, attributed to the work of Vygotsky and others, proposes that learning derives from social interaction. Children are guided by their caregivers' responses to behaviors. Individual development comes about via social processes; in the educational setting, students work together to acquire knowledge. Language and other cultural artifacts are tools for constructing knowledge. Known concepts are applied to new situations; learning produces individual mental development. Social consciousness precedes individual consciousness. Collaborative learning, teacher instruction, and attempts to imitate are means of transmitting cultural behavior.

Constructivist theory proposes that learners construct their own knowledge. The individual learner constructs knowledge through experience, either incorporating new experiences or reframing his view of the world. Teachers using this method are facilitators; students use primary sources to analyze and as they interact with other learners, work out their own conclusions rather than reproducing knowledge. Real-world tasks and reflection are aspects of constructivist learning.

TRANSMISSION OF LANGUAGE AND IDEOLOGY

Regionally - Each region of the country has unique words and expressions. Some order hoagies and others subs. Hearers may be puzzled or amused when someone speaks of hose instead of stockings.

At home - Families have unique phrases understood only within their family circle.

Internationally - Words come from other languages and become part of the shared experience.

Language is learned from vocational, religious, social, and recreational relationships.

At the personal level, each person has his own ability to use language, a pattern of grammar, pronunciation, idioms, and vocabulary called an idiolect. The idea of language as composed of idiolects contrasts with the language ideology held by most English speakers.

In hearing communities, children learn the values and traditions of their culture, its language, folklore, and religion from their parents. Social customs and rules of behavior are observed repeatedly and the values become incorporated in the lives of the children. Acculturation does not happen automatically for deaf children. Because most deaf children (90%) are born to hearing parents, sign language, deaf history, and social customs of Deaf culture are learned from Deaf peers or teachers, traditionally at schools for the Deaf. Through social interaction and language immersion, experienced visually rather than auditorily, the deaf child learns his worldview. Hearing children have more role models and typically share any minority status their parents have. Deaf children rarely share this identity with their families.

SOCIAL INTERACTION LEARNING THEORY

Vygotsky introduced the notion that social interaction as a fundamental role in cognitive development. Vygotsky rejected the Piagetian idea that children construct their understandings of the world independently. Rather, Vygotsky theorized children's development proceeds from social interaction. In a social learning context, roles are shifted. The teacher collaborates with the students and learning is reciprocal. Through social interaction, the learner gets support and, with others, participates in problem solving. The Zone of Proximal Development—the area between the student's ability to solve a problem with adult guidance or peer collaboration and his ability to perform the task independently—is where learning takes place. Benefits of this learning environment include less need for help from the instructor, improvement of learning strategies, and increased perseverance.

GUIDED PARTICIPATION

In guided participation, an experienced person works with another to help him achieve competence. The role of the social group or dyad is emphasized, rather than the individual. In this process, both individuals focus jointly on a problem. The teacher organizes the environment and provides individualized guidance. Structured experiences direct learners toward a broad goal and individuals define goals for themselves within the larger task. Guided participation extends Vygotsky's notion of the zone of proximal development ZPD. Guided participation is characterized by inter-subjectivity, meaning that purpose and focus is shared, not individual. Guided participation does not necessarily mean face to face. Emphasis is on tacit, distal, and nonverbal forms of communication.

CONSTRUCTIVISM AND CRITICAL SOCIAL THEORY

Constructivism theorizes that people create their own knowledge through experience, reflection, and assessment. Teaching practices in support of this view include experimentation, inquiry, and problem solving. The teacher addresses and builds on students' preexisting conceptions. Students take an active part in constructing their knowledge instead of passively acquiring knowledge dispensed by a teacher or textbook. A criticism of the method claims that students are always "reinventing the wheel."

Critical social theory (CST) promotes critical thinking in a multidisciplinary framework that connects theory with practice. CST views all scientific knowledge as a social construction. Inquiry focuses on the technical - ways to predict and control the natural and social world; practical - human interaction; and emancipatory bases - the freeing of individuals from physical, mental, and social injustice.

STRENGTHENING COMMUNICATION SKILLS BASED ON SOCIOCULTURAL THEORY

The goal of the activities is for learners to understand how people speak in given circumstances; to learn what expressions might be used when one is asking for directions or making an introduction or apology. A method of coming up with situations is to reflect on all the times during the day one would have occasion to speak to someone; what settings and persons has that person encountered? Other means of promoting conversation are through storytelling. A group of related pictures can be used to prompt a student to create a story, to come up with characters and dialog. Another activity poses a realistic situation about which students must make a decision; as they consider the

24

possibilities, students share their thinking out loud. Role-playing gives many opportunities to practice conversation.

NATIONAL TECHNICAL INSTITUTE FOR THE DEAF

The Center for Education Research Partnerships (CERP) at the National Technical Institute for the Deaf (NTID) promotes collaboration among national and international organizations, educational institutions, and individuals. It seeks to link research and practice so that deaf students have the best chance for success. Dr. Marc Marschark, who directs the center, says that historical approaches to deaf education don't work well. Research at the CERP is determining how deaf children acquire and organize knowledge using memory tasks and tracking eye movements. Research shows that material for deaf learners should be arranged visually and spatially. Students in mainstream settings might do better with more learning support corresponding to the individual needs of the student. CERP maintains a website, www.educatingdeafchildren.org.

PRAGMATICS IN LANGUAGE, ETYMOLOGY AND ICONICITY

The study of pragmatics explores the way in which the meaning of a word or sentence depends on its context. Elements such as time, place, and social relationship are included. Language users learn to match utterances with the situation, using appropriate form of address, listening behaviors, and protocol for taking turns. Pragmatic errors may hinder communication because they can be interpreted as rude or abrupt.

Etymology traces the development of a word (or sign), its history, meaning, and evolution.

Iconicity means that a sign resembles the thing it refers to; its meaning is conveyed in the form the sign takes. Once considered substandard language, it is now recognized that all languages are iconic, though in sign languages it is often more apparent.

INTERLANGUAGE

The second language learner uses a third language that is neither the native language nor the target language. This third language, or interlanguage, uses words and grammar rules that are not found in either language. Learners may go through a predictable series of interlanguages throughout the learning process. The learner may overgeneralize, using a rule for the target language in a situation where it is not correct. A learner may use only present tense or use a category word like flower instead of a more precise term like daisy. His speech may be simplified like that of a child when he does not know the correct form.

REFERENTIAL, SOCIAL, AND AFFECTIVE MEANING

Referential meaning - what the sign or sentence describes

Social meaning - what is revealed about the language user; a person's choice of a word or sign may identify the person's sex or where he is from

Affective meaning - conveys feelings, attitudes, or opinions through sentence structure or word/sign choice

Referential meaning is called denotation; social and affective meaning are called connotation.

Linguistic competence has to do with knowing the sounds of the language, how they work together, what combinations of grammar and meaning are possible, and what conventions govern their use. From linguistic performance, linguists draw conclusions about linguistic competence.

LANGUAGE FUNCTION AND USE OF A LANGUAGE LADDER

Language function focuses on its purpose, rather than its grammatical form. Speech becomes more meaningful when used for a specific purpose, such as asking permission, introducing someone, or expressing affection. Much of our speech serves a specific purpose. To teach language as function, the teacher creates a context or situation. The instructor also explains how to choose an appropriate utterance from among the many possibilities.

A language ladder is a tool that models various levels of expression from formal to informal. The appropriate choice depends on the situation; relative social standing, how well you know someone, and who else is listening affect the choices.

COMMUNICATIVE COMPETENCE

Communicative competence is the goal of language acquisition; to be used appropriately to accomplish communication goals. Four areas of competence are:

Linguistic competence - knowing how to use the language's vocabulary, grammar and syntax

Sociolinguistic competence - using the language appropriately in a given setting and with the people who are communicating; the speaker knows how to express and identify attitudes being expressed

Discourse competence - using language coherently over longer stretches and the ability to understand others conversations and messages.

Strategic competence - recognizing misunderstandings and knowing what to do about them; finding ways to express ideas even though not all the words in the new language are known.

IMMERSION APPROACH

In a language immersion program, the target language is used almost exclusively in the classroom. Language is taught directly through conversation, just as language is natively learned, rather than formally through learning grammar rules. When only the target language is used, there will be more input received and more attempts at communicating in the new language. Drawbacks are that instructions given in the target language many not be understood and the instructor won't know if it is the language or the concept itself that is too difficult. Grammar may not be as well developed as when taught systematically. This approach has been used to preserve heritage languages as well as teach foreign languages. Partial immersion and dual immersion are variations of this philosophy. An immersion environment may not suit every learning style.

LANGUAGE INTERFERENCE

A language learner's first language affects his production of the language he is learning. Language interference, also called cross-linguistic interference or transfer, is the deviation from the norms of either language. Interference can affect grammar, vocabulary, accent, word order, use of pronouns, tense, etc. Patterns used in the native language are transferred to the language being learned. Transfer can be either negative, resulting in errors, or positive, producing correct language production. Negative transfer is likely to be greater when the two languages differ greatly. Interference is inevitable with imperfect command of a second language and may be either a conscious choice or an unconscious one.

COGNITIVE LINGUISTICS

Traditional views held that language was isolated from other cognitive processes and understood by rules. Learners memorized arbitrary forms and learned formulas for politeness. Cognitive

Linguistics views language as interacting with other cognitive abilities and reflective of the spatial, physical, and social world. It draws on real world experience and taps into the reservoir of knowledge. Grammar is employed automatically, not as individual parts.

Pragmatic instruction can highlight subtle features of language used in interactions and increase both comprehension and production. By observing speech acts such as apologies and invitations, in which the learner is not directly involved, he has the opportunity to become familiar with the conventions used in those situations. The goal is not to conform to a particular norm, but to be exposed to a range of devices and practices.

CRITICAL PEDAGOGY IN THE FOREIGN LANGUAGE CLASSROOM

Critical pedagogy takes into account the beliefs and attitudes one usually has about a language; it seeks to develop students' consciousness of social oppression. In critical pedagogy, the relationship between student as passive and teacher as active agent is changed. The dialogical method explores experiences of both students and teachers without imposing their beliefs on the other. Culture is taught by investigating issues.

Basil Bernstein examined the distinction between everyday or common-sense discourse and formal discourse. What he called horizontal discourse is local, dependent on context, and multi-layered. Horizontal discourse is oriented to the present. In contrast, in a formal school setting, discourse tends to be vertical. Knowledge is progressive, divided by age or ability; it is hierarchical, explicit, and structured systematically. Vertical discourse is oriented to the future.

LANGUAGE ACROSS THE CURRICULUM (LAC)

In the Language Across the Curriculum (LAC), language is used as a learning tool in other courses traditionally not combined with second language learning. The idea is that learning language for a purpose improves fluency. Learning to use the new language purposefully helps students be prepared to function in a multilingual, global society. The use of LAC may range from adding a few vocabulary words to full integration of the language. Identifying appropriate materials will take effort; textbooks may not be as useful as such mass-media items as news, websites and performances. Using LAC necessitates cooperation of faculty in identifying vocabulary and other language skills that will meet educational purposes of the course. Assessment will also take a variety of forms and require additional planning.

IMMERSION, SUBMERSION, STRUCTURED IMMERSION, AND BILINGUAL EDUCATION PHILOSOPHIES

In an immersion environment, only the target language is used; simplified sentences or other types of caretaker speech may be used. The theory of immersion is, as learners are addressed in the target language exclusively, they will pick it up. Submersion, sometimes called the sink or swim approach, places students in classrooms that only use the new language, at a level of speech that is not modified for easier understanding. A Supreme Court decision in 1974 called for equal treatment of students who lack English language proficiency. Structured immersion features pullout classes. Its goal is for students to be mainstreamed; it is an expensive model and found to be relatively ineffective. In a bilingual learning environment, students use their native language to acquire a second language; there is no agreed on model. For transitional or subtractive models, bilingualism is not the intended outcome. In the additive model, the second language is added; it doesn't take the place of the native language.

CODE-SWITCHING

Code-switching is a change in dialect, tone, or language while speaking or signing, using different variations according to context. A bilingual individual may use each language in certain settings or with certain people. It is not the result of confusion, but is rather governed by rules. It is natural for deaf children who know both ASL and English to code-switch, using it as a linguistic tool.

Code-switching is believed by many theorists to be purposeful behavior, used in order to convey cultural identity, language prestige, or to negotiate power for the speaker. Some theorize that code-switching is semi-lingualism, a strategy used when neither language is known completely.

GOAL OF COMMUNICATION FOR LOTE

The overarching goal for LOTE is communication. Most course outlines include five elements in the communication goal:

Function - what students use the language for, such as greetings, conversations, expressing likes and dislikes, and making requests

Context - where the communication takes place, whether face-to-face, electronically, through video materials, pictures, and menus

Text type - the organization of language, progressing from words and phrases to short sentences, questions, commands, and idiomatic expressions

Accuracy - correct structural use of language as well as culturally appropriate behavior; effective communication that is not hindered by excessive hesitation or errors

Content - communication topics, usually including self (home, school, friends, health, leisure activities etc) and topics beyond the self (weather, places and events, work, historical and cultural figures)

GUIDING PRINCIPLES FOR LOTE

There are eight guiding principles for LOTE. The first four are:

Acquiring languages other than English is essential for all students. - All students can benefit from language learning; the skills learned translate to other subject areas and scores on standardized tests may improve.

Multiple student variables affect how students acquire languages. - Some factors that affect language learning are age, previous experience with language, learning styles and disabilities, as well as emotional environment. Variables can be addressed by using a combination of teaching strategies.

Knowing languages other than English at advanced proficiency levels upon graduation benefits students and society. - A desirable workplace skill and an asset to the community, multilingualism helps individuals cross cultural boundaries and enhance their personal lives.

LOTE programs that start in elementary school and continue uninterrupted through high school allow students the possibility of reaching advanced levels of proficiency and benefit students in other academic and social arenas. - Starting second language study early not only gives more opportunity to develop proficiency but benefits learners' understanding of self and other cultures as well.

The last four are:

Maintaining and expanding the language of native speakers benefits the individual and society. - Students with skill in other languages are valuable cultural resources, but native language ability should be increased and improved upon as well.

Students should have opportunities to develop proficiency in a variety of languages. - Less traditional languages, such as Russian and Japanese, are becoming more important in the global economy and relations between countries.

Learning languages other than English is interdisciplinary. - Second language learning techniques applied to other subjects helps reinforce learning and introduces content that may not otherwise be a part of the curriculum, such as literature.

Learning languages other than English enable students to better understand other cultures. Studying the products, practices, and perspectives of another culture helps students develop analytical skills.

NOVICE, INTERMEDIATE, AND ADVANCED LEVELS OF CONVERSING

The three levels of conversing have progressively different skills:

Novice - understands short utterances; produces phrases and sentences; detects main ideas in familiar material; knows that communicating appropriately involves knowledge of culture; knows the components and grammar that produce accurate expression

Intermediate - participates in simple face-to-face communication; creates statements and questions to communicate independently; understands main ideas of familiar topics and can supply details; understands simple statements and questions; uses what is known of the culture when communicating; uses grammar with increasing accuracy; manages social and survival situations.

Advanced- participates in casual conversations in culturally appropriate ways; explains; narrates; uses correct tense; can give the central idea; can navigate social and survival communication events; uses accurate expression by using knowledge of grammar and other language components.

AREAS OF COMMUNICATION SKILLS ASSESSMENT

At the novice level, students are expected to engage in simple conversation, respond to requests, give the main idea as well as details, identify objects, and describe and compare things. The student uses and understands expressions that indicate emotion and can express agreement or disagreement as well as basic needs. Communication skills are assessed in three areas:

Interpersonal - social interactions (including introductions), greetings and goodbyes, answering biographical questions, and expressing likes and dislikes

Interpretive - understanding simple stories and brief instructions, describing characters from a familiar video, or creating an illustration for a story

Presentational - using words, phrases and sentences to present information, giving and following directions

In addition to skills acquired at the novice level, the intermediate level student makes use of what he has learned about the culture as his communication skills develop. He has knowledge of grammar that increases his accuracy of expression. The student communicates successfully in social and survival situations, interprets instructions and announcements, and can present information on familiar topics. The intermediate student makes progress in using appropriate tense, initiating conversation, and explaining and supporting opinions. He identifies and states feelings and emotions, expresses basic needs, and knows expressions of courtesy. The intermediate student is able to compare and contrast, as well as make suggestions.

In the interpersonal mode, a student can exchange information, as well as ideas and opinions. Interpretive skills include demonstrating an understanding of a variety of topics, including literature. Presentational skills include the ability to present information on a range of topics. The advanced learner converses in culturally appropriate ways, uses past, present and future tenses, and understands most details of presented material. He copes with more difficult social and survival settings and uses grammar correctly for accurate expression. Techniques, by which a speaker may persuade, negotiate and elaborate opinions, are introduced. The student begins to be able to analyze, criticize, hypothesize, and predict; he sustains conversation and can summarize a plot.

TARGET LANGUAGE IN THE CLASSROOM

The American Council on the Teaching of Foreign Languages (ACTFL) recommended, in a position statement updated in May 2010, the target language be used as exclusively as possible (more than 90% of the time) by educators and students in the classroom, as well as at other opportunities outside the classroom. The Council's K-16 Standards for Foreign Language Learning in the 21st Century emphasizes target-language interaction as central to learning a language. Examples of strategies to maximize target language use include: comprehensible input directed toward communicative goals; comprehension checks; encouragement of negotiation among students; encouragement of self-expression; and spontaneous use of language. Increase of fluency, accuracy, and complexity should be elicited and feedback offered. While the ACTFL emphasizes reading ability, it is understood that the goal for American Sign Language learners is the ability of communicative signing ability.

COMMUNICATIVE COMPETENCE MODEL

The goal of language teaching is communicative competence. Learners gain the ability to use the language appropriately and correctly in order to accomplish communication goals. Four areas of communicative competence are:

Linguistic - competent use of grammar, syntax, and vocabulary

Sociolinguistic - ability to use language appropriate to the setting, topic, and relationships of the people communicating

Discourse - putting words, phrases and sentences into coherent and contextually appropriate conversation, speech, and other types of longer messages

Strategic - ability to overcome gaps in knowledge of the language (express ideas when the exact word or form is not yet known) recognize and repair miscommunications. Learners make use of strategies to avoid confusion and offense and communicate to the fullest level of proficiency.

HOW LANGUAGE ACQUISITION IS AFFECTED BY INTERNAL AND EXTERNAL ENVIRONMENTS

Neurological development is an obvious requirement for language learning. But environmental conditions, both internal and external vary widely. Second language learning is especially affected by qualities of environment. Quantity and quality of input, structural or immersion method of teaching, optimum usage of language, number of students, and personalities all affect learning.

30

Introversion, teacher style of correction, and whether or not questions are encouraged and students are allowed to help set goals are other factors. Motivation can help overcome external and internal inhibitions. Two types have been identified: Integrative motivation derives from a desire to interact with the community that uses the target language and is interested in the culture; instrumental motivation springs from the desire to earn academic credits or some other tangible reward such as a job. Both types of motivation may be involved in the learner's effort.

ATTITUDES

A monolingual mindset in a nation or society will affect support for learning other languages as well as expectation for success. "Foreign" language learning marks it as outside the norm and assigns a minority status to the language. Instructors' attitudes are impinged by worldview and philosophy of learning. Within the school, support for language clubs and field trips affects learning. For all, the belief that all languages are equal linguistically is important. One seeing minority languages and cultures as legitimate leads to a change in practice at every level. The foreign language classroom can have a wider perspective, carrying over into social and political arenas.

EFFECTIVE PEER ASSESSMENT AND SELF-ASSESSMENT

Alternative assessment methods need to be introduced gradually to students unused to active participation in evaluation of themselves and their peers. The rationale for alternative assessment can be discussed. In peer assessment, students must understand what they are expected to provide feedback on; they can participate in establishing the criteria and practice methods of conveying feedback. Effective peer evaluation depends on students trusting one another to provide helpful and honest evaluation; small group work can help students feel comfortable and able to provide better feedback. Self-assessment requires students to think about how and what they are learning. Self-defined and -relevant goals are necessary for students to measure their progress against. Contracts between learners and instructors are one way to set up the goals; teachers can guide students in setting realistic goals. Strategies for setting these goals must be taught through modeling and practice. Students can compare self-assessments within a group or with other kinds of evaluations, such as tests.

SCAFFOLDING

Instructional scaffolding is a teaching strategy that builds on students' pre-existing knowledge. The teacher provides individualized support, such as visuals or other well-known material, while providing tasks that enable the learner to internalize new concepts. Clear feedback is provided, as is an environment conducive to risk taking. As learners demonstrate mastery, support is decreased. Four phases of instructional scaffolding were identified by Vygotsky: the first phase offers modeling along with verbal commentary; the second phase is when the student imitates the skill modeled by the instructor, along with the commentary and the instructor offers assistance and feedback; during the third phase, the instructor offers progressively less assistance and feedback; in phase four, the student can perform the new task without help from the instructor.

CORRECTING STUDENT ERRORS

Inform students in advance of the type of errors that will be corrected; these should pertain to items that are not beyond the student's level of proficiency. Feedback should be direct and immediate, but not so as to interrupt communication. Respond to content, not just form, so the student knows you are listening, not just watching for errors. Ask students to clarify statements, providing their own paraphrase. Model correct forms by paraphrasing the student's utterance. By not automatically supplying the correct form, students learn to depend more on themselves than on the teacher. Student errors are a source of information; they reveal what the learner has or has not mastered. Note recurring errors and give feedback to the entire group.

LANGUAGE PROFICIENCY AS A LINEAR PROGRESSION

While critical points can be identified along the course of proficiency, linguistic skills do not progress in a straight line. An inverted triangle better represents the broadening of skills needed to gain proficiency. In early stages where vocabulary and phrases are memorized and repeated, less effort is needed. This stage requires less experience and practice and is represented by the point of the triangle. Later development of skills requires more practice and the ability to incorporate new grammar and make creative use of language. Advanced learners integrate cultural and linguistic skills and develop flexibility through more extensive practice and challenging experience, as illustrated in the broad base of the inverted triangle.

OBSERVATION, PERFORMANCE, STUDENT LOGS AND JOURNALS

While observation can provide useful feedback, it is not an assessment by itself. A checklist and a tally of times a behavior occurs are two ways to gather data from observation. Both teachers and peers can record this data. A performance can be a single task or event and can be used to gather data by using the criteria previously set out in a rubric. A rubric for evaluating a group project should take into account research, discussion, participation, and planning. An individually completed component should also be assessed.

Activities completed outside of class can be recorded as student logs. The information can show regularity of practice, trends, and changes in behavior. Self-recorded logs are not useful as summative assessments, but can be part of a portfolio. Journals are another means of self-reporting. Content is not appropriately used for assessment, but entries can be assigned and also included in portfolios.

PERFORMANCE TASKS

Performance tasks, that replicate challenges and situations that learners are likely to encounter outside the classroom, give students the opportunity to demonstrate strategies and solutions. The tasks emphasize the learner's strengths rather than his weaknesses. Such tasks reflect the interests of students, pose real-world communication situations, and require language to be used creatively, not by rote. Performance tasks are multi-stage and involve interaction between the learner and instructor or peers. Performance of tasks allows for self-correction. Students learn from the evaluation process, as the learner knows what is included in the criteria for evaluation. The focus is on communication, rather than on correct answers. Tasks are performed in a supportive environment and feedback is contributed by peers. Learners are also given an opportunity to reflect on their own performance.

STUDENT PORTFOLIOS

Portfolio assessment, a joint process for learner and instructor, evaluates progress over time. A student's work is collected and organized according to guidelines for inclusion. The selection is then reviewed and reflected on as to whether goals have been met and to further refine the goals that have been set. ASL learners' video portfolios record both planned and spontaneous language used for a variety of purposes and for differing audiences. Measuring achievement individually allows for differences in students. Portfolios emphasize language use and cultural understanding, as well as representing a range of performance. They emphasize what students can do, not what they can't, and document a student's progression from earlier work to later performance. Portfolios are instrumental in goal setting and measuring a student's progress. Process portfolios usually reflect formative assessment, while product portfolios usually reflect summative assessment.

APPROPRIATE ASSESSMENT FOR LANGUAGE LEARNERS

Effectiveness of testing methods is a challenge in language learning. Instructors must consider the kinds of knowledge a test can evaluate. An assessment includes gathering information, analyzing the data, making an evaluation, and produces some type of written product.

When communicative competence is the goal, alternative assessment methods provide more accurate measures of progress. A summative assessment measures progress over a predetermined period with an external standard of measurement, such as a final or midterm. In ongoing or formative assessment, students help identify criteria and recognize ways of improving their own learning. The functional ability to communicate is rated, rather than the number of right answers. Both types of assessment can be used.

RUBRICS

Checklists are easily constructed: Parts of a communication task are listed, with columns for noting completion. One limitation of a checklist is that it assesses only completion, not the quality of the work done. A rubric establishes criteria for measuring the quality of the performance and is often used with benchmarks. A rubric is usually used for generic tasks, but can be specifically formulated toward a goal. A numeric or graphic scale can be used in conjunction with written comments. Four types of rubrics are:

Holistic rubrics - emphasize what a student does well in language performance as a whole; four to six points of assessment are used

Analytic rubrics - separate categories represent separate dimensions of performance, each of which is scored separately, as not all categories have to be weighted the same

Primary trait rubrics - focus on one dimension of language performance

Multi-trait rubrics - rate three or four dimensions of the particular task.

FEEDBACK

Active feedback may take the form of a test or comprehension check. Implicit feedback makes assumptions - understanding is taken as a given when no signal of noncomprehension has been observed, for example, uncorrected utterances are taken to be appropriate. Explicit feedback can be subtle or overt; it includes questioning looks or cues. In the audiolingual approach to language learning, feedback was used to reinforce behavior - praise or modeling of the correct utterance was offered. The cognitive approach used reinforcement plus information.

Feedback is a complex issue. Instructors need to decide whether to interrupt communication or leave errors untreated; whether the error significantly impairs communication or pertains to the focus of the lesson and how to do so. Correction should not be assumed to lead to learning.

SAMPLE TOPICS FOR NOVICE, INTERMEDIATE, AND ADVANCED LEARNERS

Novice and intermediate learners can learn language, increase vocabulary, and promote conversation through any of the following topics:

- Holidays
- songs and music
- weather seasons
- times and dates
- money and numbers
- food
- businesses
- sports
- geography
- hobbies
- health
- invitations
- family

- expressions of courtesy
- numbers
- pets and animals
- clothing
- colors

- restaurants
- transportation
- events
- professions
- customs
- greetings

- biographical information
- places
- invitations

Topics appropriate for advanced learners for increased communication can include:

- government and politics
- current events
- media
- philosophical issues
- art and literature
- history
- customs
- belief systems
- travel
- environment
- technology

FLASHCARDS

Flashcards can be useful at elementary levels of learning and review. A flashcard can remind a student how to produce a sign, but is limited in its depiction of movement. Flashcards can be used in exercises at the phonological level; they can teach handshapes and prompt students to produce signs using that handshape. Partners using flashcards with each other practice comprehension and discrimination as to whether the sign or handshape is correctly produced. Flashcards do not usually lead to interactive communication as the signs depicted are "frozen" and the English gloss may be misleading as though the sign were equivalent to the English word and that word only.

MULTIPLE INTELLIGENCES

The Verbal/ Linguistic learner can interpret stories and role-play, and analyze jokes and idioms. A Logical/ Mathematical learner could collect data on how his peers spend their leisure time and compare it to that of someone in the target culture or devise questions or experiments. Kinesthetic learners can manipulate objects they learn the names for. Visual/ Spatial students can make maps, illustrations, and chart characteristics. Musical students will use songs and rhymes to acquire language. Intrapersonal learners might communicate with a deaf person through email or instant messaging and compare experiences; they will identify emotions and mediate in groups. A Naturalistic learner will go on an outing and record his experience, noting differences and similarities in those who are deaf and those who can hear.

MAKING TARGET LANGUAGE INPUT UNDERSTANDABLE

"Comprehensible input" means that the language used is at the learner's level of comprehension. While the concepts being taught are not made simpler, the language used to discuss them can be modified; presenting basic concepts in a variety of ways. Teacher-talk, foreigner talk and caretaker speech are easier to comprehend than native speaker language. Clear articulation and a slower rate of speech, along with the use of high frequency vocabulary, will assist in understanding; more time for processing should also be allowed. Target language input should be simplified; use of short sentences and simple syntax can be used. Less use of idioms and slang expressions, than would be used in ordinary conversation, is desirable. Comprehensible input is necessary for the achievement of proficiency.

COMPREHENSIBLE INPUT

Stephen Krashen proposed that language is acquired when students take in language slightly beyond the level of ability. A phrase can be altered slightly to provide new information while still relating to what is known and is, therefore, comprehensible. Teachers must be aware of students' current level of comprehension. Communicative support can be provided in visual props, for example, to give clues to context. Instructional strategies guide students from cognitively undemanding situations to context-imbedded communication; along a continuum to context-reduced exchanges in which a student must synthesize information and understand abstract concepts. Students are challenged by, but not overwhelmed by, new material. The comprehensible input theory has been extended to output as well - learners are given opportunity to use the skills they have acquired.

GOALS PUT FORTH BY NOSTRAND, SEELYE, AND OTHERS

Rather than amassing a list of historical and geographical facts or cultural trivia, language learners are taught critical skills to support intercultural communication and understanding. To make a study of culture purposeful, learners will develop curiosity about and empathy toward members of the target culture. Through instructional activities, they learn that:

Social class, age, gender, place of residence, religion, ethnicity, and other social variables affect speech and behavior

Thoughts and actions are culturally-conditioned

Convention significantly shapes behavior

Society allows certain options whereby people can try to satisfy their basic needs

Generalizations made about a culture are to be examined and research carried out to support or deny them.

INCREASING TARGET LANGUAGE USAGE

To limit the tendency of students to use speaking instead of signing:

Permit voicing part of the time - allow students to ask questions at the beginning of class, for example, then switch to voices off. A signal can be set up—a certain location in the room, a flag or some other object—that indicates a student wants to use his voice.

Use written English to maintain a "voices off environment," provide language support by giving directions on an overhead or computer projector.

Set up alternate days, or sessions where voicing can be used or establish a lab time for questions.

BILINGUALISM IN THE DEAF COMMUNITY

Although most Deaf people are bilingual to some extent, using both ASL and English in various modalities, there is much variation. For Deaf children raised in Deaf families, ASL is their first language. A deaf person may use one language in the home and another at school. Others learn ASL as adults and may or may not belong to Deaf culture. Skill in reading and writing English may be marginal to fluent.

Some Deaf people are fluent in both languages. In a bilingual society, not every individual uses two languages with fluency. Where two languages are used in the community, one of the languages usually takes a majority position, this is typically the one used in education.

TEACHERS' ROLE IN THE ACCULTURATION PROCESS

Frustration over the inability to communicate and understand other aspects of cultural exchange can result in a certain amount of culture shock. A student's own worldview and self-identity undergo changes when they come into contact with these other cultures. Teachers facilitate the change in students from seeing the Deaf as "other" to seeing those who are like him. Common ground must be discovered and analogies made. From an outer, less personal, circle of environmental (tangible and physical) elements to more private traditions and symbols, the inmost layer of a culture discloses the values and beliefs held in that culture. Each person is respected as an individual, albeit each with a different history and life experience. The differences are recognized, valued, and must be embraced by the teacher if students are to accept them, as they most often learn this by example.

PERIODICALS FOR AND ABOUT DEAF PEOPLE

There are a variety of periodicals for the deaf community:

American Annals of the Deaf - oldest professional journal about deafness; focuses on education, language development and teacher training

Deaf Life - independent magazine by and for the deaf published since 1988

DEAF USA - includes news of interest to the deaf as well as professionals in the field

Deafweekly - free weekly e-zine

The Tactile Mind - annual publication of literature and artwork

The FRAT - published by the National Fraternal Society of the Deaf

Hearing Health - provides resources for the deaf and hard of hearing and to health and education professionals

The Journal of Deaf Studies and Deaf Education - published by Oxford University Press

Odyssey - the magazine of the Laurent Clerc National Deaf Education Center at Gallaudet University

World Federation of the Deaf News - the magazine of WFD

TEACHING CULTURE THROUGH LITERATURE

One of the limitations of literature as a way of teaching culture is the tendency to make generalizations from a book that describes only a part of a subculture. Literature is often set in the past. Experimental or surrealistic works are not likely to reveal cultural patterns; a limited range of insights is presented and may cause misunderstanding. Literature can illustrate cultural patterns that have been already identified through social sciences and make them more memorable. Folklore can be used for instructional purposes, as it is handed down through generations and explains traditions and customs. Through literature, students can develop empathy, especially as minority and mainstream culture characters interact.

GLOBALIZATION AND LOCAL COMMUNITIES

Some writers warn that as globalization minimizes the borders between communities, local language practices, and other cultural aspects are becoming not only homogenized, but marginalized. Local knowledge, it is feared, is swept away by the language majority who decide curriculum and teaching methodology. Globalization brings major changes in economies and political power. Communities may be pressured to abandon traditional practices in favor of modernism. Global standards for language challenge local varieties as substandard. Specialists and those with local knowledge are in conflict; alternate literacies are suppressed; indigenous culture is misunderstood and not appreciated. Assimilation into the dominant language is assumed. Pedagogies unsuitable for the situation are used. Power is maintained over minority communities. It is especially difficult for societies with no written language to resist the powerful majority.

Fostering respect for diversity

Literature exposes students to experiences and perspectives they would not otherwise learn about; values and beliefs are infused in these texts. Literary texts are a rich source of authentic language and a wide variety of literature exposes readers to various dialects. It can also teach students about their own culture. Literature by minority authors can be included in the curriculum throughout the year; inclusion of other than European American authors needs to become more frequent. Traditional classic literature often does not connect with the cultural identities of students.

Literature about deaf people can reveal stereotypes and show what's important in a particular society. How women or different ethnic groups are portrayed is very telling about the author, as is who in the story has money and power. Children's books and the body of work represented in a library can also heighten sensitivity to multiple cultures.

DEVELOPING ACADEMIC LANGUAGE

Scaffolding offers strategies for helping students learn to use known vocabulary in the context of academic subjects, as well as the unique and technical vocabulary of the content area. Language can be simplified by using shorter utterances in the present tense and avoiding idioms. Students can be asked to choose from among answers or complete a sentence before they are required to generate longer sequences. Use of organizational and visual tools, such as outlines and charts, can aid learning.

Theme studies in which learners are actively involved provide meaningful context. The theme can be introduced in a book and expanded upon with demonstrations. Direct explanation, expansion, and comparisons increase comprehension. Students connect with the text by making predictions, drawing on what they know, and by relating personal experiences. A project such as a poster or performance can be completed as a group.

AUTONOMOUS AND PRAGMATIC MODELS OF LITERACY

In the autonomous model, meaning is embedded in the text. Readers extract the information with no attempt to interpret or negotiate meaning. Pragmatic models assume that meaning is created as readers interact with the text.

Classroom talk differs from other conversation. Patterns have been established - namely the initiation-response-evaluation form - before children even start school. Teachers and parents ask questions they already know the answers to, "what's that?" for example. Sections of discourse are often unrelated and jump from topic to topic, in keeping with instructional goals. Classroom discourse lacks the transitions that occur in regular conversation. The discourse patterns may not be familiar to students in minority cultures.

VOICE-OFF POLICY

For deaf people to be heard, voice is used as technology. Interpreters voice for the deaf, but other technology can allow members of the deaf community to speak. A "voice-off" policy is sometimes used with children for whom ASL is being established as a first language: voices are turned off and sign language is relied on for communication. In meetings where both deaf and hearing are in attendance, a voice off policy gives hearing participants the opportunity to experience what deaf people face continually. In this setting, voice does not overpower sign language. To communicate in visual mode means sight lines have to be maintained.

DISCOURSE ANALYSIS

Discourse analysis examines the quality of coherence in communications beyond the length of a sentence. Language does not assume meaning and purpose from its linguistic forms alone, but from the interaction of the participants. Coherence is relative to context including the participants' knowledge, the situation, the culture, and the role and relationship of the participants. No longer attempting to find linguistic rules for generating possible sequences and sentence boundaries, theories and techniques of discourse analysis examine text in context. Conversational principals, functional analysis, pragmatics, schema and genre theory, and the study of cohesive devices are elements of discourse analysis.

Diglossia is when a speaker uses variation of language in different social contexts. One type of language may be used in formal contexts, while another is used in conversation. One form of language may be considered more prestigious than the low variety.

COMMUNICATING WITH DEAF PEOPLE WITH MINIMAL LANGUAGE COMPETENCY

Minimal language competency is not necessarily a function of intellect. There are a number of reasons why a Deaf person may not be fluent in ASL or any language. To facilitate communication, use ordinary gestures, pantomime, and rudimentary homemade signs. One can point to an object or person, use pictures, or other available props. Be sure to confirm understanding before proceeding to another topic. Watch the person's facial expressions. A nod doesn't necessarily indicate the person understands; it may be a signal for "I'm paying attention." Try to establish a baseline fact to build on: use consistent tense, careful reference to time, repetition is helpful, avoid finger-spelling; above all, treat the person with respect.

INTERACTING WITH THE DEAF COMMUNITY AS STUDENTS AND AS INSTRUCTORS

Interactions with the Deaf community require humility as awareness of the new culture is brought forward. Much interaction is needed to develop fluency. For students, make clear that deaf people do not need or want 'help'. Interacting with the Deaf community is a resource for teachers to improve their ASL skills and experience professional growth. Through their frequent contact with the Deaf community, instructors help their students gain respect for the culture. Ties between the language learning program and the Deaf community are essential. Teachers should be comfortable with native users of ASL and reflect on their own motives, as well as be informed by new research, teaching materials, and methods.

EXCITEMENT IN THE ASL CLASSROOM

Both students and prospective visitors should know what is on the agenda for a planned visit. Students can prepare interview questions and practice conversation in terms of appropriate language and social requirements, such as greeting style and eye contact. Deaf visitors should know if they will be asked to tell a story, as well as the students' level of proficiency. They should be offered reimbursement for their time and expertise. Both parties should also be aware of the purpose of the lesson.

Members of the deaf community can serve as language consultants. As they share humor or stories from their own culture, students can become more natural in their interactions with members of the deaf community. Lessons are reinforced through planned activities.

RESEARCH THAT PROVED ASL TO BE A TRUE LANGUAGE

Before research proved otherwise, signing was thought to be gestures, a substandard means of communicating used by the deaf. William Stokoe, a teacher at Gallaudet, began a systematic study of sign language and discovered its linguistic structure. Sign language was discovered to have its own syntax, phonology, and morphology. By developing a notation system, Stokoe was able to demonstrate its features. Although it did not record some features of ASL such as nonmanual signals, the system has been used and modified by researchers. Stokoe's dictionary of American Sign Language became an important reference work. Since his groundbreaking work, the study of ASL linguistics has become a recognized research discipline and American Sign Language is used in deaf education.

ADDING NEW SIGNS

American Sign Language grows and changes like any language. New ASL signs often have iconic associations, but they always hold to the conventions of ASL. New signs are needed for new inventions or concepts; signs change as society changes. Such signs are often mimetic, such as the sign for (computer) mouse. DOLLAR was previously signed as though it were a coin, now the sign is symbolic of a bill; TELEPHONE used to be two objects, but the sign has changed; signs that are now one word were formerly phrases.

Initialized signs are sometimes added to the lexicon. Used abundantly in manually coded English systems to differentiate words in a family, such as theatre, drama, and perform, many initialized signs are not accepted as ASL. Compounding is another way signs are added to ASL.

TRADITIONAL EMPHASIS ON LANGUAGE LEARNING

In the past, language instruction was less about acquiring the language than learning about it, emphasizing grammar and pronunciation. Today the focus is on proficiency, specifically the development of survival skills in communication and applications in the community and global society. Learners get as much exposure to the target language as possible so that they gain the ability to function in social interactions and discussions. Instructional methods are proficiency-oriented and homework assignments might include interviewing or videotaping, writing a skit, or demonstrating some cultural aspect of the deaf community. Content is connected to other subjects instead of treated separately. Native language and culture is compared with the language and culture being learned.

AREAS THAT SIGN LANGUAGE RESEARCHERS AND SPECIALISTS WORK IN

Besides interpreting, sign language specialists work together with speech and language pathologists as resources in schools. Vocational rehabilitation and mental health fields provide many other opportunities to work in the field of visual/ spatial language. Globalization will bring increased research opportunities to sign language history and structure, the acquisition of sign language, and studies in how the brain processes sign language. As links between speech and hearing and other sciences are established, improved tools for assessment and classification will need to be developed. Patterns of change in language will be further documented by researchers and measurement techniques for spatial frequency, along with other properties, will continue to be explored.

FLUENCY IN ASL TO THE USE OF CLASSIFIERS

Learning to correctly use classifiers in ASL is an area that second language learners find difficult to master. English does not use classifier morphology; ASL uses classifiers extensively in conversation and storytelling. Classifiers combine a handshape that indicates the class of noun with a second morpheme to show location or movement. Ability to create classifiers that are syntactically correct and comprehension of classifiers are essential to fluency in ASL. Fluent signers use a classifier about once every minute. Classifiers make signing more efficient by streamlining expression and eliminating the need to repeat detail. Instruction at every level should incorporate activities that practice the use of classifiers.

Second Language Acquisition

USING THE INTERNET TO TEACH A SECOND LANGUAGE

The Internet is a powerful source of authentic materials and makes it possible to interact with the world using:

Electronic mail, conferencing and messaging capabilities

Electronic lists or discussion groups - protocols for their use must be observed when participating

Electronic journals - articles are not only timely, but often link to further references.

World Wide Web - its multimedia nature and interface with other services makes the Web the broadest, most powerful use of the Internet

Streaming audio and video - connects students to native speakers and provides a virtual target language environment

Access to remote databases and libraries

Online courses can augment classroom instruction and make it possible to communicate with other students via programs like Blackboard or WebCT

SUPPORT MATERIALS FOR THE LOTE CLASSROOM

Resources to enhance language acquisition in the LOTE classroom should include general classroom equipment and materials such as instructional software, instructional and cultural videos, as well as access to the Internet and email. Sign language dictionaries, pictures, illustrations, and transparencies should also be included. Manipulatives will include flashcards with numbers and vocabulary and objects to represent foods and other items (either real or plastic). Puppets and other props to facilitate role-play are also needed. Authentic materials from the deaf culture will include newspapers and websites specifically for the deaf, books and poetry written by deaf authors, videos, advertisements or samples of assistive technology devices, information on cochlear implants and hearing aids, and material from deaf sports or theater events.

USING ENGLISH IN THE LOTE CLASSROOM

In the LOTE class, English is meant to be used as a survival tool. Since the goal of instruction is language proficiency, the target language should be used in the classroom. At the novice level, English may be used to teach culture and compare languages. As proficiency increases, students will present projects in the target language, rather than English.

Teaching grammar in the LOTE class is not an isolated goal. Students' language levels as well as their ages are taken into account when planning. Instructional methods should be chosen according to how the grammar helps meet the goals of communicative language. Accommodations for students with special needs will have to be considered in both regards.

TEACHER-CENTERED AND LEARNER-CENTERED MODELS

In the teacher-centered model, the teacher is active and responsible for transmitting information; the learner is passive and listens. This model is familiar to many teachers and requires less preparation; all the students do the same activity. Not all students will be involved in the learning process.

In a learner-centered model, both student and teacher are active participants and share responsibility for learning. Language is learned for specific purposes, not just learned about. Goals are identified by teachers and students working together; causing preparation to take longer. Teachers must connect curriculum to the real world. The dynamic classroom may seem chaotic or out of control, but the content of activities as well as their time limits is fully planned.

FOSSILIZATION

Selinker proposed the notion of fossilization in reference to the stagnation that occurs in the learning of a second language. A student may continue to acquire vocabulary, but the conceptual understanding of that vocabulary does not develop further. Fossilization is signaled by reoccurring errors and a lack of progress in competence. As many as 95% of second language learners fail to achieve the fluency they have in their first language. Some have argued a critical period hypothesis - that fossilization is inevitable when language is learned after a certain age. There are different classifications of fossilization: phonological fossilization - errors in pronunciation persist; morphological fossilization - misuse of inflectional morpheme and article; syntactic fossilization - most typical, errors in tense; semantic fossilization - use of language forms that do not express the intended meaning; pragmatic fossilization - inappropriate language use.

Fossilization is caused by both external and internal factors. Both the learning environment and subconscious processes can inhibit learning of a new language. A main factor in fossilization is language transfer - the transfer of language rules from L1 to L2. More specific elements have been identified: training transfer - informal learning during which errors are not corrected, such as in so-called street learning; learning strategy - both overall and explicit methods adopted by the learner such as incomplete rule application or overgeneralization; communication strategy - simplification of the target language, or paraphrasing to avoid grammar; overgeneralization - applies a grammatical rule too broadly.

STEPHEN KRASHEN'S "AFFECTIVE FILTER" HYPOTHESIS

The "Affective Filter" hypothesis is one of five hypotheses in Krashen's theory of second language acquisition. Affective variables such as confidence, motivation, and a good self-image play a role in success in second language acquisition. The affective filter, when it is high due to low self-esteem, anxiety, or low motivation, forms a mental block and hinders language learning. When embarrassment and self-consciousness are alleviated, the affective filter is lowered, optimal input occurs, and learning is facilitated. Krashen's natural approach, created with Tracy Terrell, calls for meaningful interaction with sympathetic native speakers that don't force production or corrections. Krashen's published work was widely accepted in the 1980s.

STAGES OF SECOND LANGUAGE ACQUISITION

The five predictable stages of second language acquisition as identified by Krashen and Terrell in 1983 are:

- Stage I: Pre-production is the silent period. Learners know some vocabulary and can duplicate responses, though without understanding. Much repetition is needed.
- Stage II: Early production may last as long as six months; vocabulary of 1000 words and one or two word phrases have been memorized.
- Stage III: Speech emergence simple phrases, sentences, questions, and conversations are possible.
- Stage IV: Intermediate fluency; more complex sentences, opinions, and thoughts can be shared.
- Stage V: Advanced fluency; language proficiency takes from four to ten years to achieve.

FUNCTIONAL-NOTIONAL APPROACH TO SECOND LANGUAGE LEARNING

Functional-notional is one of the communicative approaches to second language learning. Functional relates to communication and notional relates to meaning. It proposes that equipping students to use the language is not accomplished by teaching grammar, but focuses instead on how language is used. Learners get the opportunity to express authentic communication based on three main factors: the functions; the situation; and the topic being discussed. The Signing Naturally series of ASL teaching materials uses the functional-notional philosophy.

Criticism of the functional-notional approach says that it is an unrealistic method that overlooks other aspects of language learning; every situation cannot be predicted or made valuable to every student.

CULTURE ASSIMILATORS, CULTURE CAPSULES AND CRITICAL INCIDENTS

Culture assimilator - an interaction between a person from the target culture and the native or other cultures is described. Participants are offered choices as to what the actions or words used mean, followed by discussion.

Culture capsules - a custom or tradition in the target culture is described along with contrasting information from the native language culture. Visual information can be used to support the discussion. Two or three related capsules form a culture cluster.

Critical incidents - also called problem solving, describe situations where a decision must be made. Students make their decisions independently, then compare and discuss their answers; critical incidents typically arouse emotion about the issue.

LANGUAGE LEARNING STUDENTS PARTICIPATING IN THE DEAF COMMUNITY

Students should understand they will not be assimilated into Deaf culture and may not force themselves into the deaf community. They can seek to make friends with deaf people and are usually welcome to attend deaf cultural events. Discretion must be exercised: a whole class shouldn't try to attend a deaf club meeting. Deaf athletic groups welcome hearing students at tournaments. Casual social gatherings, such as silent dinners, may be appropriate places to interact with members of the deaf community. Common interests, such as sports or hobbies, should be sought. An appearance by a traveling theater of the deaf may afford an opportunity to meet deaf performers. The overarching task of the ASL learner who seeks association within the deaf community is to show respect for the language and its users.

LEARNING ASL OUTSIDE THE CLASSROOM

Defining success as mastery of rules and making good grades keeps the focus on the student. Help them to see success as making the language useful and envisioning what they can do with the language in the future. Explore specific possibilities and name different tasks. Students can be asked to evaluate their own progress. Are they able to perform the tasks they have identified? Encourage spontaneous expression of ideas.

For students who say they don't plan to use the language, have them imagine scenarios, such as asking for directions or giving assistance to a native speaker. Studying deaf history, plays and performances by native language users and conducting interviews are possible strategies for piquing interest.

Teaching Sign Language

TEACHING ASL AS A FOREIGN LANGUAGE

Accepting ASL as a foreign language requirement is becoming more widely accepted in schools. Those who have argued against its validity use the following reasons:

- The belief that ASL is a manual representation of English and not a true language.
- ASL is American and doesn't therefore qualify as a foreign language.
- ASL is not important in international affairs.
- ASL users do not have a distinct culture has been widely believed.
- ASL literature, because it lacks written form has not been readily accepted.
- Some have feared that the popularity of ASL would keep students from studying more traditional languages.

These objections can be answered by the fact that American Sign Language is a complete and natural language among the many signed languages in the world. It is not derived from English and its users have a distinct culture and history, including poetry and performance arts.

ASL COURSES VS. FOREIGN LANGUAGE COURSES

States differ in their recognition of American Sign Language as a foreign language. Courses in American Sign Language have taught a manual version of English (Manually Coded English or MCE) or Pidgin Sign English (PSE). These systems do not qualify as, or fulfill the requirements for, a foreign language course. ASL has been offered in Speech, Education, or Communication Disorders departments rather than in foreign language departments, making it harder to receive foreign language credit or transfer credit. One reason for this is the limited number of qualified sign language teachers. ASL instructors need formal training and experience in second language pedagogy, as well as proven proficiency. Curriculum, materials, and assessment tools for the ASL classroom are unique.

VARIATIONS IN SIGN

Differences in signs can be attributed to communities with ethnic, regional, occupational, and socioeconomic distinctions. Because of segregation, signs that originated in black residential schools, such as those for "white person" and "pregnant" are not the same as those used by white Deaf signers. Deaf students coming to the US from Mexico learn to mix ASL and LSM (Lengua Senales de Mexico). Signers who have more contact with the English language tend to use more English word order and fingerspelling. New Yorkers, it has been noted, keep their fingers straight when signing M and N as opposed to other signers who curl the fingers. Dominant methods of education such as oralism, Total Communication, or a bilingual approach, and whether teachers are native ASL users or not, add variety to ASL. Older signers will usually sign differently than younger.

CULTURAL AND LINGUISTIC TOPICS

Typical knowledge and skills associated with learning a second language include studying the culture, geography, and history of selected regions or countries. Students of American Sign Language don't have a specific location on which to focus, but can identify social, cultural, and economic changes that have affected the deaf community, notably the changes in school setting. Regional variations in ASL can be explored, as well as art, literature, and drama, which are each a large part of deaf culture. ASL students have the unique position of learning a visual language, one with no historic written counterpart. Geographical aspects of deaf culture will be less informative

44

than that of other language groups, but historical events and figures are extremely relevant to the culture of deaf people.

DEAF LITERATURE

A broad variety of ASL literature should be used and include not only works written by Deaf authors, but also film, video, and live performances. Appreciation for the variety of Deaf literature in its several languages and modalities should be part of ASL instruction. Genres of ASL literature include oratory, folklore, and performance art. Oratory includes videotapes made from films produced a century ago that have historic significance, as well as speeches at graduations and other ceremonies, as live examples. Folklore includes ABC stories, jokes, and narratives. Performance art is sometimes available on video; Deaf writers and poets, using English, express Deaf culture and identity. These make aspects of deaf culture more accessible to students not yet fluent in ASL.

CLASSROOM ARRANGEMENT

In order to learn a visual-gestural language, high quality videotaping equipment is essential for both practice and assessment. Cameras and television monitors are needed as well as knowledgeable media personnel. The language lab should include as large a collection as possible of videotapes of both ASL and Deaf culture. Locally produced videotapes are also necessary to provide help in learning local dialects; they can also cover topics not included in commercial productions. Because the study of signed languages has a shorter history than that of spoken languages and many aspects are currently being investigated, interesting research articles and books should be available. A third consideration for the classroom is the seating arrangement. Visibility is essential and students should arrange their seats in a circle or semicircle to ensure each person is able to see everything they need to.

VIDEO MATERIALS

ASL Access makes available a large selection of videos that include history, biographies, translations of classic literature, stories, and poetry. Magic Lamp Productions in Venice, CA has another extensive library of videos. DawnSignPress creates and publishes books and DVDs that teach and document Deaf culture and American Sign Language. Their goal is to preserve the works of Deaf people in arts and literature as well as produce the latest contributions; they seek to raise the standards in education. Sign Media is a leading producer of high quality materials for teaching and learning American Sign Language and all aspects of Deaf culture.

INSTRUCTIONAL VIDEOS

Instructional videos have a number of advantages including:

- Cost-effectiveness
- Appealing and suitable for students with different learning styles
- Lessons can be scheduled at any time or can be easily used by a substitute teacher
- Allows lessons to be reviewed for clarification or replayed for students who missed them
- Comprehension skills are increased by exposure to a variety of target language users
- Cultural aspects may be accessed via videotape

Drawbacks of instructional video include:

- The need for video technology and the lack of interaction and feedback between learners and instructors
- The teacher cannot control the content

- The subject matter may not accommodate required standards or go along with the projected syllabus
- Overuse of instructional videos may foster passive learning

Instructional videos can supplement the curriculum by providing a variety of language models as reinforcement of classroom lessons and as a way to view aspects of the relevant culture that cannot be otherwise accessed. Video-based programs can also be used temporarily when a qualified teacher is not available. Video instruction can present native language users as a resource for classes at higher levels of fluency. Follow up activities based on the video give opportunities for target language practice and can be tied into other curriculum areas. Further, activities based on video instruction can be incorporated school wide as multicultural learning events.

PRINTED MATERIALS

While texts or manuals are invaluable for looking up unfamiliar or forgotten signs, there are obvious limitations in presenting a three-dimensional subject on paper. Directionality and order of movements can be confusing or ambiguous. The grammar of ASL and the use of idioms are also not easily depicted in sign dictionaries. Signing with contextual appropriateness requires knowledge of deaf culture. For example, a different sign will be used for FISH when used as a noun instead of a verb.

Printed materials can be used to increase vocabulary and encourage the use of language. Examples include flashcards, pictures of animals and people, maps of countries and local geographical areas, even menus and advertising. Information found in newspapers, especially current events, can be used to promote dialog. Sequenced pictures are especially useful in practicing storytelling.

LANGUAGE TEXTBOOKS WITH AUTHENTIC LITERATURE

While language textbooks are a good source of language input, they tend to be form-centered rather than meaning-centered. The dialog and characters central to texts tend to be generic and unrealistic. Lists of personal data are often included and activities call for students to respond to surface-level information. The reading process is not intuitive or natural, nor are the conversations. The books use simple vocabulary, which comes across as artificial.

Authentic literature is more likely to use realistic language, as it is meant to be read by native speakers. An interesting story also increases motivation. Literature should be age-appropriate. Real literature provokes discussion and response that require critical thinking skills. Authentic literature is often used in college-level foreign language courses. To find and research effective material takes more time than teachers usually have available; students can help find materials.

LEFT HANDED SIGNER

A signer who is left-handed will use his left hand as his dominant hand, using it for all signs made with just one hand and also for fingerspelling. The right hand forms the base in signs such as CUP while the left hand forms the shape of the cup. Signs made with the left hand will be a mirror-image of right-handed signs. CHILDREN, for example will be signed progressively to the left. An exception will be made in giving directions such as TURN RIGHT when the hand will be moved in the actual direction to avoid confusion. It is important for the signer to use the dominant hand consistently, not switch back and forth, to avoid any confusion.

It is not uncommon for a signer to use just one hand temporarily while the other is holding something. Physical limitations may also require the use of one-handed signing.

BUILDING CONFIDENCE

Starting with the least threatening environment, move gradually to the place where students can present individually with confidence. Provide well-demonstrated materials that can be practiced alone at home. Have the class practice together as a group, facing the front; or solicit volunteers from more outgoing students. Be sure that students know the names of their classmates. Pair students and increase group size gradually to get them used to larger and larger audiences. Arrange students in different pairs and groups to get them used to being in front of constantly changing audiences. Play games or other activities in a circle. Be sure students know they can ask for help and have the option to pass when they don't know the answer. Have groups come to the front, then gradually smaller groups and eventually, individual students.

LEARNING STRATEGIES

Some learners can identify the best way to go about a specific task and are flexible enough to try different strategies; they expect to learn. Other students find it difficult to know which strategy will help them accomplish a specific task; they have few strategies to choose from and would rather stick with a strategy that isn't working than try something new. Such a learner doesn't gain motivation and doesn't expect to succeed. Many students who learn to use more effective strategies develop increased confidence and responsibility for their learning.

Students can practice various strategies and become aware of their value, knowing which ones lead to success. Teachers can identify and build on strategies students use and help them expand the range. Teaching learning strategies can be both implicit and explicit.

ENGAGING STUDENTS WITH A VARIETY OF ABILITIES

Focus on forms that are applicable to a variety of functions; role-playing can be used extensively. Outside activities, like a trip to the mall, where students describe passersby to each other help to introduce language for physical characteristics and distinctions. In the classroom, make use of visuals. Model phrases for students to repeat and modify and continue to build on the known phrase. Students can work in pairs, with the more advanced learners supporting learning in those less advanced. Small groups can discuss a problem and devise strategies for solving it. Let students take guesses at word meaning. Ask students to rate whether they know something well or aren't able to understand at all. Scaffolding techniques minimize failure by providing opportunities for student success in a supportive environment.

Linguistics of American Sign Language

GLOSS AND LEXICAL BORROWING

Gloss is a representation of ASL in written form, not a verbatim English translation. Appropriate English words that correspond to the signs are chosen and written in small capital letters. Nonmanual signals are written over the sign glosses as well as markers for tenses and plurals as well as to preposition indicators. Fingerspelled words are shown by dashes between the letters.

Lexical borrowing is the adoption of words from other languages. It results from contact between languages. The form of the word or sign usually changes so it more closely resembles the native language. Meaning may also be broadened or more limited than in the original language. ASL takes the names of other countries from their own sign languages.

INDIGENOUS SIGNED LANGUAGE

The signed language used in Martha's Vineyard from 1692 to the middle of the twentieth century was used by both deaf and hearing inhabitants. It is probable that the Vineyard sign language was introduced by immigrants from England. Many children from Martha's Vineyard attended the first school for the deaf in Hartford.

A natural signed language was used in France in the 1700's. Desloges wrote about the signed language he and other deaf people used in Paris. Both Epee and Gallaudet recognized that the deaf used a natural language among themselves, though both failed to recognize the grammar of the signed languages and introduced modifications.

SEMIOTICS, CITATION-FORM SIGN, ICONICITY AND IDEOPHONES

Semiotics - the study of signs and symbols; it analyzes the nature and relationships of signs in language. Branches include syntactics (grammar), semantics (meaning), and pragmatics (those features that depend on context).

Citation-form sign- the description of a sign that would appear in a sign language dictionary

Iconicity - the form of a symbol depicts some aspect of the item represented. Iconic symbolization is not cross-linguistic. Different aspects of 'tree,' for example, are chosen in other sign languages.

Ideophones - sounds are symbolic; they evoke images and sensations through sound. Also called expressives or mimetics, ideophones are rare in Indo-European languages, but used a great deal in African languages.

SUBMERGENCE OF ICONICITY

The iconic or representational aspect of ASL signs tends to diminish over time; the transparency of the physical aspect or activity is lost as the sign evolves. An example is the sign for HOME, which in the past used two distinct signs (EAT and SLEEP), now uses one handshape and two contacts on the cheek. Grammatical processes also tend to suppress iconicity. Intensification of the sign SLOW to mean VERY SLOWLY changes the sign to a short, rapid movement. The sign for YEAR loses its iconicity when it is modulated to mean EVERY YEAR. The centralization of some signs has lessened their iconicity, such as that for HELP: in the past, the forearm was lifted as if taking someone's arm to help; now the dominant hand pushes up on the nondominant fist in the center of the signing space. The tendency toward symmetry also tends to submerge the iconicity of signs.

HISTORICAL CHANGES IN SIGN FORMATION

Over time, articulation is more limited to the hands; body movements for some signs have been eliminated. A normal signing space has become established: signs tend to move in and toward the line of bilateral symmetry and upward to the hollow of the neck, the center of the signing space. Many two-handed signs have become one handed and there has been a tendency toward symmetry; hand configurations and orientations have become assimilated and transitions smoothed, resulting in fluidity. GOLD is an example of a sign evolved from two separate signs. Sign families have been developed that use a bent V, or bent middle finger handshape for related signs. LIKE, formerly signed with the index and thumb touching, now uses the bent middle finger.

SIGN LANGUAGE STUDIES JOURNAL

The first journal of its kind, *Sign Language Studies* was started by William C. Stokoe in 1972 to provide a publishing outlet for work on signed languages. It disseminates the latest findings in language research and publishes scholarly articles and essays. Topics include semiotics, linguistics, anthropology, Deaf culture, and deaf history. The journal helped sign language become a field of serious academic research.

American Sign Language was not identified as a language because it was believed that language was based on speech. Sign language was thought of as pantomime or gestures, dealing with the concrete and avoiding the abstract. It was believed that sign language had no grammar, as well as being derived from English and universal.

CLASSIFIER PREDICATES AND LOCATIVE VERBS

Classifier predicates consist of a movement root and classifier handshape together. The movement root can show a process of movement (a car driving by), a description (as in a pile or mound), or the movement can be a contact root. The hand has a downward movement, but the contact root does not describe movement or shape. It means BE-LOCATED-AT. The classifier handshape combines location (represented in three-dimensional space), orientation, movement, and nonmanual signals. ASL uses classifier predicates to create new signs. A classifier handshape can represent a class of objects, such as vehicle, size or shape of something, or be an instrumental handshape, showing how the hand holds an object.

Locative verbs also represent a location in three-dimensional space. An example is HURT, placed at a specific area on the body. The handshape in locative verbs, unlike classifier predicates, does not have independent meaning.

SUBJECT-OBJECT AGREEMENT

In English, word order and certain pronouns indicate which word is the subject and which is the object. The verb doesn't generally include such information. In ASL, many verbs include this information, either in the location or orientation of the verb, sometimes both. Orientation of the verb HATE, for example, tells who the subject is by the direction the palm faces. With the verb HELP, the location tells who both the subject and object are. The verbs GIVE and ASK use both location and orientation to show subject and object. Some verbs give the object information first, such as INVITE. The verb starts at the location of the object and moves to the location of the subject. Reciprocal verbs in ASL, such as LOOK-AT-EACH-OTHER, include two subjects and two objects. The verb TELL does not include information about the subject; a separate sign is required. Plain verbs, such as LOVE, require signs for both the subject and object.

INITIALIZED SIGNS

Initialized signs use a manual alphabet handshape sign. While there are many initialized signs used in ASL, they should not be overused or put into practice arbitrarily. Signs that substitute an initial handshape have to use an appropriate place of contact. DUTY and WORK, for example, contact the base hand differently. Many initialized signs are used in manually coded English systems. FAMILY and CLASS are examples of initialized signs that have become part of American Sign Language. Some initialized signs can be traced back to old LSF, such as the C hand-shape used in TO-LOOK-FOR. It comes from the French chercher. ASL name signs are predominantly initialized. Certain handshapes, D, E, R, T, and W, are used almost exclusively in initialized signs. Academic ASL uses more frequent initialization and fingerspelling.

CLASSIFIER HANDSHAPES

There are seven types of classifier handshapes used in ASL:

- Whole entity morphemes - refer to an object as a whole, a person, or thing
- Surface morphemes - that represent narrow, wide, or thin surfaces or wires
- Instrumental morphemes - represent holding an object or instrument, such as a cup, camera, or scissors, as it is used
- Depth and Width morphemes - represent layers, the depth, or the thickness of things like pipes or snow; these also indicate various widths of stripes
- Extent morphemes - represent volume, amount, or an increase or decrease in something, such as a stack of paper
- Perimeter-shape morphemes - represent external shapes, such as a picture frame or clump of grass
- On-surface morphemes - represent large groups or crowds

ASL VS. ENGLISH PRONOUNS

English pronouns distinguish between masculine and feminine - he, his, she, and her, for example, as well as between subject and object. The subject pronoun is he; the object pronoun, him. ASL pronouns do not indicate masculine or feminine, or differ between subject and object. The meaning of a pronoun is determined from context. The location of a pronoun sign serves an important function: while a person can point to the left or right to indicate another person, that same location must be maintained throughout the conversation. Determiners modify nouns, indicating whether the noun is specific or one of a particular class. English uses a, an, and the; ASL points with the index finger, before, after, or with the noun. Determiners signed simultaneously with the noun use the passive hand. The direction the finger points does not carry meaning. To sign "the girl is silly", GIRL (the determiner) SILLY is signed.

CONDITIONAL SENTENCES

A word such as "if" indicates a conditional sentence. ASL also uses IF and SUPPOSE, but conditional sentences can be constructed without those words. By using nonmanual signals including raised eyebrows, a tilt of the head, or sometimes a short pause, the expression is understood to be conditional. Compare "If it snows tomorrow, the meeting will be cancelled" with TOMORROW SNOW (with conditional nonmanual signals) MEETING CANCEL. When the object of a sentence can be moved to the front, topicalization occurs. Nonmanual signals are used - raised eyebrows, head tilt, or a short pause. An example of a sentence that is topicalized is BABY (with topicalization nonmanual signals) MOTHER LOVE, as a way of expressing the mother's love for the baby.

SEQUENTIALITY

In the spoken word, phonemes are combined in a particular sequence. To recombine the segments would result in another word with a different meaning. Signed languages, although they are primarily simultaneous, do have an element of sequentiality. It was long believed that signs were holistic and unable to be analyzed as parts. Stokoe identified cheremes in signs as corresponding to phonemes in spoken language. Beginning in the late 1970's, linguists suggested that ASL phonology contains a sequential aspect; they distinguished movements and holds in the production of signs. The sign IDEA consists of a hold (the I handshape at the eye), a movement forward, and another hold. The components, as in spoken words, do not carry individual meaning; they are combined into a whole unit that then has meaning.

SIGN PARAMETERS

The five parameters of a sign are:

- Handshape - letters of the manual alphabet and numbers are the most frequently used; some are modified, such as a flattened O or open F
- Palm Orientation - the direction the palm faces - up, down, left, or right
- Location - most signs are formed near the head and neck to be easily seen; location often contributes to the meaning - signs that indicate feeling are made near the heart
- Movement - repetition may be used to indicate frequency, size, and plurality or differentiate between a noun and a verb; direction toward or away from self indicates who is the recipient of the action
- Nonmanual Signals - convey additional information in the same way tone of voice adds meaning to spoken language; changing any of the components changes the meaning of the sign

BASIC OBJECTS; SUPERORDINATE ITEMS; AND SUBORDINATE ITEMS

ASL has fewer signs for superordinate and subordinate terms than for basic objects. Three levels of categorization are expressed in ASL as follows:

- Basic objects - share attributes with other members of the category; have primary ASL signs, such as a hammer
- Superordinate - members of the category do not have the same attributes; the category is expressed by using a series of basic object signs, prototypes of the category—hammer, saw, and screwdriver for the category "tools." The movement of the signs is reduced and there are minimal transitions between signs.
- Subordinate - the sign for the basic object is used together with a detail or specification of size and shape, such as FOOD CHAIR for dining room chair. Subordinate items may also be expressed as a compound - the primary ASL sign with a Size And Shape Specifier (SASS); SAW plus a mimed shape signifies a hacksaw.

DISTRIBUTION, DEGREE AND RECIPROCITY

ASL signs use morphological processes to communicate frequency, duration, and other aspects of verbs. The morphological processes in ASL mark semantic distinctions that include distributional aspect, temporal aspect, degree, and reciprocity. These distinctions are marked in many spoken languages. ASL differs dramatically from English and other spoken languages particularly in the spatial mechanisms used and the way the mechanisms are combined.

Emphasis, sarcasm, anger, degree of intensity, and emotional states are conveyed in ASL by facial expression, mouthing, and upper body position. Signs made without appropriate expression will be perceived as monotone, if not misunderstood altogether. ANGRY, without accompanying facial expression, could indicate sarcasm. Facial expression corresponds to the tone or pitch in a spoken language. To convey intensity, a sign may be reduplicated or, if it is a short word, fingerspelled for emphasis. Large space articulation or exaggeratedly slow movements are ways of signifying degree.

SYMMETRY CONDITION AND DOMINANCE CONDITION

Symmetry Condition - when making a two-handed sign, both hands use the same handshape and type of movement, as in HAPPY and MAYBE.

Dominance Condition - if a two-handed sign uses different handshapes, only the active hand moves; the passive hand does not move. The passive hand is usually one of seven basic handshapes.

Lexicon is the vocabulary of a language, individual words or signs. A minimal pair of words differs by only one sound in the same position, pat and bat, for example. Minimal pairs of signs share three out of four parameters; the signs for APPLE and CANDY, for example, differ only in handshape. Nonmanual signs are one of the five basic parts that make up an ASL sign; they are the facial expressions and body movements necessary to produce the sign correctly. Nonmanual signals can indicate negation, question, or imperative; facial expression has distinct rules and timing.

LOCATION

Location, a part of all ASL signs, may be a location on the body or in the space around the signer. The location serves a number of functions:

- The location of the sign may be simply articulatory, or how the sign is made. The location in this case does not have independent meaning.
- Space may indicate phonological contrasts. In this case, the location of the sign changes its meaning. SUMMER and DRY are examples.
- Morphological use of space shows, for example, the direction of a verb from one person to another.
- Morphological space can indicate continual or repeated action, aspectual markers.
- Space can be used to indicate a pronoun or place, called referential function.
- Space can be locative, showing the location of a person or object.
- Space can indicate frame of reference such as east, west, north or south.
- Space serves for narrative perspective as in storytelling that involves several characters.

ASSIMILATION, METATHESIS AND PHONOLOGICAL PROCESS

Assimilation - a sign is modified by taking on the shape, location, or movement of another sign. Most commonly the handshape or movement is modified to blend with another sign more easily. A sign may be reduced to one movement rather than be repeated.

Metathesis - the initial and final location of some signs can be reversed. An example is the sign for DEAF, which ordinarily touches first the cheek, then the jaw. A number of signs that touch both sides of the chin, such as RESTAURANT, FLOWER or TWINS can be reversed. Most signs cannot use metathesis without changing the meaning.

Phonological process - the way in which parts of signs influence each other and may occur in different orders. Examples are movement epenthesis, where a movement segment is added between two signs or a hold is deleted. Metathesis and assimilation are both phonological processes.

DISTINCTIONS THAT SHOW WHETHER A SIGN IS USED AS A NOUN OR A VERB

Verbs usually use a single large movement while the related noun is signed smaller and with a double movement. FOOD, for example, is signed with a double movement and EAT, as a single movement. PET, when used as a verb, is signed with a single movement; the noun PET uses a double movement, as does the word PHONE when used as a noun. LEISURE and HOLIDAY use a single movement and VACATION uses a double. Adding the agent or person marker changes a verb, such as TEACH, into a noun, TEACHER. Directional verbs, such as GIVE or LET, incorporate the subject and object by moving toward or away from the signer. Locational verbs indicate the area of the body referred to, such as HURT signed near the head or tooth to indicate HEADACHE or TOOTHACHE.

ANALYZATION OF HANDHSAPES FOR FREQUENCY OF USE

Researchers have categorized ASL handshape configurations as Fixed Prime and Variable Prime. Studies have indicated that as many as 70% of all signs are made with six handshape configurations. Features, such as compact hands (no fingers extended), broad hands (with three or more fingers extended), full hands, concave hands (cup shape), dual hands (with middle and index fingers extended), index, radial and ulnar hands (having to do with the index, thumb or little finger), have been analyzed as to whether or not they are used with the prime handshapes. Touch, cross, and spread hands describe other features. Some researchers classify handshapes as "selected fingers" and "aperture". Spoken language phonemes include distinctive features such as voicing and place. Fewer than twenty features distinguish the sounds of spoken language. In both languages, phonemes lack meaning without context.

COMPOUNDING

When signs are produced in sequence, phonological rules such as the following may be applied:

- Movement epenthesis: a movement segment that does not change the meaning is added between the two words that form the compound, as in THINK SAME.
- Noncontact holds between two signs are eliminated, such as with LOOK STRONG.
- Assimilation: a segment takes on the characteristics of a segment before or after it. The handshape for THINK changes to the handshape of the sign MARRY in the compound translated "believe".

As in English, knowing the meaning of the two signs is not enough to know the meaning of the compound word. The words BLUE and SPOT, for example, have different meanings, until compounded to mean "bruise".

In English, a compound word is formed when two words are joined to create a new word, as in 'bookcase'. The stress on a compound word is usually on the first word; the compound word has a different meaning than the two words from which it is formed.

ASL applies three morphological rules to create compounds:

- The first contact rule - The first or only contact hold is kept; when two signs form a compound, the hold of the first sign stays, if it has one. If it does not, the contact hold of the second sign stays.
- The simple sequence rule - Internal movement, or repetition of movement, is eliminated. An example is the ASL compound GIRL SAME. The repetition of SAME is eliminated.
- The weak hand anticipation rule - The weak hand appears with the necessary handshape while the active hand produces the first sign. GIRL SAME illustrates this rule as well.

COMPRESSION OF TIME IN COMPOUND SIGNS

When two signs are compounded, the duration of the compound is shortened. The movement of the first sign is reduced and weakened in time and length and loses its stress and repetition. The second sign also loses repetition, but retains its normal stress, or may take on added stress. There is also a change in the way one-handed signs are made when the second part of the compound involves a two-handed sign. Rather than the base hand remaining at rest in the first, one-handed sign, the two-handed sign is anticipated. For example, in the compound BLACK NAME, meaning "bad reputation," the base hand of NAME appears throughout the sign. Transition between compounded signs is reduced; signs may be made closer together, for example, increasing fluidity. In time, the identities of the signs forming the compound may disappear. REMEMBER, a composite of KNOW and STAY, is an example.

YES/NO QUESTIONS

In English, a yes/no question places the verb before the subject (Is John home?). The speaker's voice usually rises at the end of a question. In ASL, yes/no questions do not have a particular word order, so nonmanual signals —raised eyebrows, widened eyes, a possible forward tilt of head and body as well as raised shoulders, and a hold of the last sign—are necessary to convey a question.

English wh- questions (using where, who, when, what and why) are usually in verb-subject order. The speaker's voice often goes down at the end of a wh- question. ASL also uses the wh- words, but with specific nonmanual signals. The head tilts and eyebrows squint; shoulders may be raised and the signer may lean forward slightly. ASL uses a wiggling X handshape at the end of the sentence to check what another person is saying or when the signer is surprised at what he has been told.

HOW NOUNS ARE DERIVED FROM VERBS

Some English verbs are used to create nouns from the same words by placing the stress on different syllables. The nouns are often stressed on the first syllable and the verb on the second as in convert and convert. The stress changes the sound of the vowel. Another pattern for changing verbs to nouns in English is by adding the suffix -er.

In ASL pairs of verbs and nouns differ in the movement of the sign, CALL and NAME, for example. The basic structure of the verb is repeated or reduplicated to form the noun. English and other spoken languages use affixation, adding prefixes or suffixes (bound morphemes), to verbs to create new units. ASL tends to repeat the segment of the original form.

COMMUNICATING TIME

Tense in English is communicated by adding the morphemes -s and -ed. It may also use another form, such as saw or brought. Time in English also uses lexical items such as yesterday, tomorrow, etc. Time in ASL has been explained in terms of an imagined time line. Present is signed near the torso, future farther away in front of the signer, and past in the area over the shoulder. ASL also uses lexical items such as now, later and recently. UP-UNTIL-NOW and FROM-NOW-ON seem to make use of the imaginary time line. Signs such as YEAR and WEEK are oriented toward either the past or future and may incorporate numbers. Habitual time is indicated by repetition, rather than signing EVERY and WEEK. The sign FINISH, often translated as "past" is not properly used as an equivalent of the English morpheme -ed.

RHETORICAL QUESTIONS AND NEGATION

Although rhetorical questions use words such as "why," "who," and "where," they use different nonmanual signals than the wh- questions. Raised eyebrows and a slight shake or tilt of the head signal that a question is rhetorical and doesn't expect an answer.

English sentences are negated by using the word "not" as in "She is not home." A sentence in ASL is negated by shaking the head and possibly squinting or frowning. The sign NOT is sometimes used for emphasis.

As in English, commands or imperatives in ASL often delete the subject, though it may occur after the verb as a pronoun. Nonmanual signals include direct eye contact and a possible frown.

MORPHOLOGY

Morphemes combine to form words in different ways across languages. In various languages, the same concept is expressed in few or many words. Chinese words are nearly all formed of single morphemes; it is an isolating language. English has many more words made of multiple morphemes (a synthetic language), and Inuit language, said to be polysynthetic, has still more. ASL is also polysynthetic; although it has single-morpheme words, ASL can combine more morphemes in its words, in different ways, than English. A root word in ASL can have morphemes added to it to indicate the subject, the object, and the frequency or tense.

Three components of morphological processes are manipulations of forms in space: planar locus; geometric arrays; and direction of movement, referring to sideways, up or down, space or plane, points, arcs, circles, and lines)

Six components of morphological process are temporal qualities of movement: onset/offset; rate; tension; evenness; size; and contouring, referring to movement and hold, intensity, muscle tension, straight, circular, continual or elliptical, fast or slow, elongated or abbreviated

Two components interact with other dimensions: cyclicity and doubling of the hands, referring to singular or multiple articulations and simultaneous or alternating movement of the hands. Simultaneous inflections create complex patterns of meaning and can be ordered alternatively.

MORPHEMES AS BOUND AND FREE, AS FORMS AND PROCESSES

Morphemes that can occur by themselves as independent units are free morphemes. The English word cat and the ASL sign CAT are examples of free morphemes. Bound morphemes do not have meaning alone; they must combine with other morphemes.

In English, verbs are transformed into nouns by adding the suffix -er. The verb walk becomes the noun walker. The morpheme in this case is a form. When the verb insult becomes the noun insult, by changing the stress from the second to the first syllable, a new word is created by a process. In ASL, the verb SIT becomes the noun CHAIR by a morphological process, a change in movement.

GRAMMAR

No longer viewed as the primary goal of learning a language, the study of grammar supports total language instruction rather than existing as a separate piece or an end in itself. There is still controversy over whether grammar should be taught explicitly or implicitly. Grammar lessons not given in a useful communicative context don't appeal to the majority of learners. Considerations for its teaching include the age, education level, and learning style of students. Word order, sentence structure, and other elements may need explicit instruction when they are unlike the learners' native language. Grammar concepts can be introduced by a brief explanation then practiced in context. When students are introduced to an oral or written narrative, they can discuss a grammar point occurring frequently in the narrative. Drills may be appropriate in some situations.

LAYERING OF NONMANUAL MARKERS

Nonmanual markers send clear and separate information using the upper face, lower face, head, and shoulders. The lower face sends adverbial and adjectival information such as "mm" with the lips pressed together or puffed cheeks for communicating big, fat. The position of tongue, lips, teeth, and cheeks is learned and controlled. Upper face and head nonmanuals carry separate information. Edge markers indicate the end of a phrase and domain markers are held for the duration of a phrase. It is the spatial separation that makes layering of signals possible. Head tilt, body thrust, eye blinks, eyegaze, etc can be articulated independently for complex combinations. The use of nonmanual markers differs across signed languages.

LAYERING OF MORPHEMES

By layering, more than one meaningful unit of information can be sent at the same time. Manual layers in ASL can be articulated in a number of ways. The two hands may function independently, one as an indexer, for example. Classifiers use layering; morphological information is laid over a basic lexical item to efficiently transfer information. Articulation of one piece of information must not interfere with other units. Nonmanual layering affects grammatical and affective purposes by varying onset and offset. Abrupt onset and offset perform syntactic functions; gradual onsets give affective information. These features are not used in the same way in spoken communication. The timing and abruptness of a headshake, for example, do not convey linguistic meaning in spoken language. Layering is proved not to be a function of modality because signed English cannot be made efficient by layering.

DISTRIBUTIONAL ASPECT OF ASL VERBS

Inflections are used with ASL verbs to distinguish between acts that are whole or separate, at what time and in what order they occur, and whether the action pertains to each individual, certain individuals or groups, or to anyone. Using GIVE as an example, distribution can be exhaustive (something is given to each one or each one gave something to me). Inflections may show distribution as pertaining to a closed group or a collective object or series. Inflection for allocative determinate means separate actions occur at distinct times with respect to specified recipients; allocative indeterminate inflection shows that separate actions occur with respect to unspecified recipients. Each process has specific properties of movement.

NUMERAL INCORPORATION

The handshape of a sign changes to express a number while the location, orientation, and nonmanual sign remain the same. Numeral incorporation has two morphemes: the segmental structure (holds and movement, location and orientation), which does not change, and the handshape, which indicates a specific number. Numeral incorporation is common in ASL and used with the signs WEEK, MONTH, DAY, DOLLAR AMOUNT, etc. Numbers greater than ten are usually signed separately. In signing "nine weeks", the numeral would be incorporated; "fifteen weeks" would be communicated in two separate signs. Signs that incorporate numerals often have characteristic location, movement, and orientation.

METHODS DEVISED TO WRITE ASL

Because more than one movement is visible at once, sign language cannot be written in a single line of script. American Sign Language researcher William Stokoe devised a system for writing sign language: inventing the words dez, sig, and tab to denote the sign's location, handshape, and motion. Stokoe's notation system lacked the capability of including important aspects of signs, such as nonmanual signals. Liddell and Johnson introduced a sign notation system based on the movement-hold model.

Devised by Valerie Sutton to write dance choreography, then adapted to record sign language, SignWriting includes the five components of a sign: handshape, movement (including contact), nonmanual signals, and location and orientation of the palm. The set of symbols is capable of recording any signed language. Software to type the signs is also being developed.

FINGERSPELLING

Bede's Ecclesiastical History mentions use of the fingers to represent the alphabet as long ago as the 7th century. Dactylology, or the use of a manual alphabet, can be traced to the 15th century where monks used it for various reasons, including teaching deaf children. Bonet's 1620 book describes teaching deaf students using a manual alphabet. From the first deaf school in Paris, where fingerspelling was used to teach spelling and the written language, the manual alphabet spread to the United States and other countries. For a time, the Rochester Method, which used fingerspelling exclusively, was used in the Rochester School for the Deaf in New York state. Films from the beginning of the 19th century record the use of fingerspelling and it is used similarly as it is today. ASL users fingerspell more than users of other signed languages do.

LEXICALIZED FINGERSPELLING

While full fingerspelling produces each morpheme distinctly, in lexicalized fingerspelling the separate signs become word-like and tend to follow the rules of ASL that limit the number of handshapes. In lexicalized fingerspelling:

Signs may be deleted when there are more than two handshapes in a sequence.

The location may change to include grammatical information.

Handshapes may change in anticipation of the next handshape.

Movement may be added naturally in transitioning between holds.

Orientation of the palm may change.

Movement may be reduplicated as in HA and NO

The second hand may be used for emphasis.

Location of the hands can indicate relationship.

DEVELOPING SKILL IN FINGERSPELLING

Sign language students often experience frustration in learning to fingerspell, and even more difficulty developing fluent receptive skills. Time and commitment are needed to acquire both expressive and receptive skills. Repetitive motion injury (RMI) is a possible consequence of intensive practice; one should watch for swelling, numbness, tingling, redness, burning sensation, and loss of range of motion. To prevent injury, warming up and only practicing 20 minutes at a time are recommended. If a student's hand hurts, he should temporarily stop practicing. He should not switch hands as the non-dominant hand is at greater risk for RMI. Ways to exercise and stretch to prevent RMI include shrugging shoulders, opening and closing fists rapidly, and moving wrists in clockwise and counterclockwise circles. One should consider whether other hobbies or activities involving repetitive routines are contributing to stress. Ice can be used to reduce inflammation.

WORD ORDER OF ADJECTIVES AND ADVERBS

ASL usually, though not always, places adjectives after the noun. Adverbs, usually the same sign as an adjective, are placed before the verb; modal verbs follow the main verb. Numerals occur after the noun in ASL, a rare pattern in spoken languages. Time can appear before topic.

Instead of a sign for and, ASL combines phrases separated by a short pause or identifies items as part of a list. There is a sign for or, but it is usually indicated with a nonmanual signal - a slight shoulder twist. Facial expression, together with shoulder shifts similar to or, indicate the conjunction but. The manual sign is used more often in Signed English than in ASL.

ORGANIZING GROUPS OF SIGNS IN LEXICAL CATEGORIES THAT SHARE SYNTACTIC PROPERTIES

Major lexical categories are nouns, predicates, adjectives, and adverbs. In this group, new words are easily added. Minor lexical categories are determiners, auxiliary verbs, prepositions, conjunctions, and pronouns. The words belonging in these categories are fixed.

Each category's set of morphological and syntactic frames (the sign's position with respect to bound morphemes that can be attached and relative to other classes of sign in the same frame) is unique. Bound morphemes are not attached to nouns; determiners indicate plurality. Meaning of adverbs is often incorporated into the predicate or adjective sign. Progressive tense of ASL predicates is indicated by adding the progressive morpheme, such as READ with repeated movements.

MORPHOLOGY, PHONOLOGY AND SYNTAX

Morphology is the study of the way words are constructed out of the smallest meaningful units. A morpheme that can occur independently is called a free morpheme. Bound morphemes must occur with others. For example, the suffix -er cannot occur by itself, but when added to another morpheme, it creates a new word.

Phonology in sign language is concerned with the handshape, location, orientation, nonmanual features of signs, and how signs are organized and structured. It is the study of the smallest parts of language that do not have meaning.

Syntax is the study of the way sentences are constructed and how they relate to each other. It is grammar, the set of rules for making sentences.

FORMAL AND CASUAL DISCOURSE

American Sign Language used in an academic or business setting is usually at a slower pace and uses a larger signing space than in casual settings. Formal ASL signing is fully executed, clear, and uses two hands. Discourse markers are different in formal signing, such as body shifting to indicate change in speaker with more exaggerated movement and indexing; in contrast, casual signing may use just a head movement. Casual signing makes more use of assimilation, one-handed signs, eye gaze for indexing, as well as incorporating colloquial expressions. Nonmanual signals may be used alone in casual signing situations. Rhetorical questions are more likely to occur in formal discourse than in casual.

RULES FOR WORD ORDER AND THE ROLE OF NONMANUAL SIGNALS IN ASL SYNTAX

Simple sentences can be in Subject-Verb, Subject-Verb-Pronoun or Verb-Pronoun order. Verb-Subject is ungrammatical in ASL. Topicalization, where the object is the first element in the sentence, is common in ASL; it is marked by nonmanual features. When sentences are not in Subject-Verb order, they are marked. The Pronoun Copy Rule says that repetition of the subject as a pronoun is accompanied by nodding. In an imperative sentence, the verb can come at the beginning or end.

The word order can be the same in different ASL sentence types - nonmanual markers change the meanings. Yes/no sentences do not follow a particular word order; nonmanual signals are required. Declarative sentences are not marked by one particular nonmanual marker.

DIALECT, DISCOURSE AND LANGUAGE REGISTER

Dialect refers to the varieties within a language that a particular speech community uses. It is often a regional variation of the standard language. A dialect uses distinct pronunciation, vocabulary, and grammar. Dialects are variations within a language, not separate languages. Speakers who use different dialects of the same language can usually understand one another. Some languages may be mutually intelligible in written form, but not when spoken. Dialects at either end of a continuum, widely separated geographically, may not be mutually intelligible.

Discourse refers to the use of language beyond the sentence. It is the study of the functions, norms, and structure of language. Discourse can be structured by turn-taking, topic, social function and skill level.

Language register is language used depending on where and when a conversation takes place. In an informal setting, two-handed ASL signs are often made with one hand and sign choice may differ. In a formal setting, the signer might use rhetorical questions and a larger signing space.

CONTACT LANGUAGE, PIDGIN AND CREOLE

Contact language is a simplified language that develops among speakers without a common language, usually retaining features of the existing languages. Significant changes to grammar often result. Contact sign is a blended form of American Sign Language and English, used for communication between deaf and hearing people. A pidgin language is a type of contact language that uses words from one or more languages to meet the specific needs of the speakers, as in the marketplace. Pidgin is simplified, having fewer rules, and does not become the primary language. Creoles are pidgins that have become the primary form of communication. Pidgin Sign English (PSE) blends American Sign Language and English as a way of communicating between the deaf and hearing.

MAINTAINING BILINGUALISM

Speakers of one language may relocate to where another language is spoken for economic or other reasons. Invasion and colonization are other causes of bilingualism. National languages are sometimes introduced. Education and culture are reasons for bilingualism: Latin was once the language of education throughout Europe. Before the Russian revolution, French was the language of culture and education. Intermarriage, urbanization, and enforcement of official languages are other factors. Some deaf children become bilingual, learning ASL from parents or in school.

When two languages are used in the same location, one of them may disappear. In some countries, two languages are known and used by everyone. One may be used in school and government, while the other is used at home. Separate languages can coexist in the same area for long periods, as in the use of French and English in Quebec.

DEAF SIGN LANGUAGES, ALTERNATIVE SIGN LANGUAGES, AND ARTIFICIAL SYSTEMS

Natural languages developed by deaf people and used in Deaf communities are deaf sign languages. Signed languages have been carried to other countries by educators and missionaries. Languages other than those natural ones are often used in schools where deaf students are educated. An alternative sign language is one developed and used for a special purpose by hearing people. Examples are sign languages used by Native Americans, Australian aboriginal women, and Christian monks. An artificial system represents spoken language and may borrow signs from Deaf sign language, but uses the grammar of the spoken language. Artificial systems have been devised for educational purposes, including the Rochester Method, Cued Speech, and the Danish Mouth-Hand System.

CUED SPEECH

Developed by Dr. R. Orin Cornett in 1966, Cued Speech is a visual system that makes each spoken syllable comprehensible. It uses handshapes to distinguish between consonants. Various locations near the mouth distinguish between vowels, thus making lipreading more effective. Cued Speech is used with over 50 languages. It supports the use of cochlear implants and development of articulation skills, as well as giving a complete phonemic model of language. Cued Speech can be learned quickly and fluency achieved in just months. It allows parents to use full vocabulary and range of expression rather than communication that is limited to known signs. Cued Speech can be used in combination with other methods. A major drawback of using Cued Speech is that its use is not as common as other ways of communicating, nor as widely accepted by professionals. There are relatively few skilled transliterators.

REGISTER OR STYLE VARIATION

Register has previously been defined as the level of formality, ranging from intimate to progressively more formal style up to the formulaic discourse of the courtroom, or "frozen" register. Other models categorize language use by province (the setting), status (social relationship), and modality or purpose. Field, mode, and tenor of discourse have also been examined. Register in ASL has often been described as a function of diglossia, a high and low variety of signing used for formal and casual situations. The idea of a "linguistic repertoire" holds that a speaker uses a variety of languages, dialects, and occupational varieties in several speech communities. Unexpected register is often used in humor. Culture and subculture define speech styles and taboos. Interpreters need to be able to use the intended register. Students of language need to learn what forms are appropriate in certain situations.

MANUAL CODES FOR ENGLISH

Signed English systems are not taught in an American Sign Language class, but it is important for students to know about them. Understanding the difference between American Sign Language and Manually Coded English (MCE) will help dispel myths and misconceptions about ASL. The student will begin to understand that ASL words cannot be translated word for word to English. One objection has been that exposure to manual codes will make learning ASL more difficult, but making the distinction between the two and unlearning wrong ideas about ASL as a language will be an asset. Students should also know, as an aspect of Deaf culture, that people may have strong feelings about MCE. Some Deaf people resent its place in education and view it as corrupting their language. Thoughtful discussion about the place of Manually Coded English is part of learning both the language and culture of the Deaf.

SIGNED ENGLISH SYSTEMS AND ASL

Signed English is the manual representation of English - one sign for each word in the same order as spoken English. Signed English systems, beginning in 1969, were developed as educational tools to help children learn English. In Signed English, or Manually Coded English, a spoken word accompanies each manual sign. In addition to the sign for a word, such as "book", a marker can be added to signify the plural. Markers are also used to indicate past tense, comparison, or negation.

Many signs incorporate an initial letter to differentiate between different items within a category, such as car, bus, and truck; all of which are signed the same in ASL.

Signed English uses signs already established in ASL, when they can be translated to one English word, such as girl or summer. Signed English systems rely on fingerspelling to communicate words for which no sign has been developed.

SEQUENTIAL NATURE OF ENGLISH WITH THE SIMULTANEOUS PRODUCTION OF SIGNS

The sequencing of segments is a fundamental characteristic of spoken language. Rules govern the organization of sound segments in their order and combination. Although the sequential nature of speech is its predominant character, simultaneous features do occur. ASL is organized sequentially at the syntactic level to form phrases and sentences and in fingerspelling. The individual units of American Sign Language, however, are not a sequence of separate and distinct configurations; the handshape and movement are simultaneous, making the sign a continuous whole. Both spoken and sign language are composed of a set of recurring elements, but words are organized sequentially and signs combine components taken from several spatial dimensions simultaneously.

GESTURE AND SPACE

Gestures (using the hands as articulators) are an intrinsic part of American Sign Language. Gestures are linguistic when they carry meaning. Gestures supplement spoken language and some researchers suggest gestures can be viewed as part of language. In signed languages, space is used formally - people or things are located in a space and maintained in that position by the signer for the duration of the topic. Locations can be designated with nonmanual as well as manual signals.

In spoken languages, space between the listener and speaker is not considered part of the linguistic structure. Gestures, however, use space to locate objects and show relationships between objects. Study of the use of gesture and space explains their necessity and sufficiency between users of different languages. Some define gestures as prelinguistic elements and signs as formal linguistic devices.

INFLECTIONAL AND DERIVATIONAL MORPHOLOGY

The study of words formed from the same lexical base is derivational morphology. Grammatical markers added to show tense, person, gender, and number are the subject of study in inflectional morphology. English makes rich use of derivations but less of inflectional variation; ASL makes extensive use of inflection. ASL verbs are varied internally in ways that are not easily expressed by simple English phrases. English inflections are either lexical or phrasal. English uses affixes - morphological processes that tend to be linear. Instead of adding sequentially to signs, ASL superimposes contrasts in space and time; inflection affects the movement of signs.

Mutual actions in ASL are indicated by a reciprocal inflection. English uses reciprocal pronouns, such as each other and one another. Other ASL inflections include indexical, number, distributional aspect, temporal aspect, temporal focus, manner, and degree.

Sociology and Cultural Anthropology

TEACHING ASL CULTURE

Cultural understanding of users of ASL is unique in several ways. Only recently have the Deaf even been recognized as having their own culture. Part of the deaf cultural heritage includes the face that formal training in ASL has a short history and that the language has been suppressed and ridiculed. Signed languages share characteristics with spoken language, but the visual aspect changes everything. Understanding the rules for social interaction, best learned directly from native ASL users, is of paramount importance. As with any language learning experience, differences within a culture may be more important to explore than differences between cultures. Even within the classroom, multiple cultures are represented. Instead of a list of traits, glimpses of another culture are gained by insights into how a person makes sense of the world. When studying ASL culture, one should ask: Who do deaf people think they are? How do they see me?

Culture is more broadly defined than in the past. No longer a list of facts, customs and perceived characteristics, culture is thought to influence all of human behavior—thoughts, communications, values, expected behaviors as well as their ability to be transmitted to succeeding generations. Instead of culture study tacked on to language learning, it is now viewed as integral. The study of culture necessitates putting oneself in the place of the other; learners examine their own beliefs to gain insight into a society. Language cannot be taught as a code governed by grammatical rules; language and culture are inseparable. Cultural practice is revealed in the small details in the lifestyles of ordinary people, not just the elite.

TRADITIONAL UNDERSTANDING OF CULTURE AS "HIGH" AND "LOW"

In the traditional view, culture was understood as formal (art, literature, philosophy and music) or popular (low). Language study was for the purpose of appreciating and understanding the high culture; popular culture did not merit study. Learning the language had priority over culture learning.

The contemporary view understands culture as the beliefs, values, knowledge, practices, and behaviors shared by a group of people. Culture is integrated with and influences language teaching because cultural norms and values are reflected in the way language is used and structured. As identified by the National Standards in Foreign Language Education Project, 1999, "the exquisite connection between the culture that is lived and the language that is spoken can only be realized by those who possess a knowledge of both."

WESTERN CULTURE VALUES TRAITS

Western culture values individual preference, directness and straightforwardness. Communication focuses on an accurate exchange of information; ideas are debated, solutions offered and argued. These attributes have been taught throughout life. But in other cultures, less competitive, assertive behavior is valued. It is not considered appropriate to volunteer, take risks or offer doubt or criticism. Cooperation is valued and passivity is a sign of respect. An indirect manner of speaking is deliberate; decisions take longer. Even people who claim to value individualism may behave in collectivist ways. The Q and A model of Socrates is not the way of all cultures; some expect teachers to impart wisdom, not act as equals. Western ways are unrefined and seem inconsiderate to those whose cultural heritage has instilled a pattern of maintaining human relationships above effective and economical communication.

62

ETHNO-LINGUAL RELATIVITY

Ethno-lingual relativity is a perspective from which the learner is willing to see the contrast of his culture with that of others in culture and language patterns. It has been proposed that this perspective makes it easier to learn a new language. This learner can recognize culture boundedness and has tolerance for ambiguity. Learners understand that languages do not translate literally. Thoughts are expressed by language arbitrarily; one way is not inherently superior to any other. In the classroom, learners explore and reflect on their own culture and the target culture in a neutral space. Distinctions between their own and the new culture are not judged. Students learn that cultures are not monolithic; they will find their own voice in the second language community. Authentic insights can be gained from native language speakers.

TRANSMITTING CULTURE THROUGH LANGUAGE

Culture does not remain static; people must learn from one another across generations. Changes that take place between a grandparent's lifetime and a grandchild's show cultural shifts in artifacts, values, and language. Language does not transmit all of culture, yet language and culture are inseparable. Language carries culture through literature, art, poetry, jokes and stories, magazines, newspapers, radio and television, movies, and the Internet. These tell the history of a community and its relationship to the world. They demonstrate the way Deaf people live and what they value. Cultural values, and obviously Deaf culture, are not written. Feedback about behaviors, both positive and negative, teaches children to fit within the culture.

ACCULTURATION THEORY AND THE INPUT-INTERACTION-OUTPUT (IIO) MODEL

The Acculturation Theory, proposed by Schumann, suggests that successful acquisition of a second language depends on how close the learner comes to the target culture. Social and psychological distance must be reduced to provide opportunity for interaction. Attitudes, knowledge, and behavior are modified as learners see themselves as part of a new language group. Motivation is a factor affecting intake of language; the need for comprehensible input is increased by the need for acceptance.

The Input-Interaction-Output (IIO) model is an interactive model of second language acquisition. In the IIO model, grammar develops through interaction. Input, considered the most important factor is apperceived (new L2 information), comprehended (matched against existing knowledge), and may be assimilated. The next step integration, stores new information, forms hypotheses, and confirms existing hypotheses. Output is the manifestation of acquired language and is necessary for language development; it tests hypotheses and elicits feedback, enhances fluency and processing ability.

THREE-LEVEL FRAMEWORK FOR TEACHING

"Because language and culture are inseparable, it is not necessary to focus overtly on culture."

Culture is taught implicitly, but the relationship between culture and language is complex. It cannot be assumed that students are learning cultural knowledge and skills. Learners benefit from well-planned lessons, also. Intentionally teaching culture can help overcome stereotypes as well as make it possible to assess learning and provide important feedback, a component that has been overlooked. Second language learning has global implications as it develops intercultural communication.

Stern's foundational level is based in the social sciences - anthropology, sociology and sociolinguistics. Applied linguistics, level two, brings theory and research together. The third level is the practical level, which is the sociocultural component. The framework places language and culture in the societal context.

HIGH CONTEXT AND LOW CONTEXT

High context societies are groups of people closely connected over a period of time. In these societies - family, friends at school, small religious congregations, etc. - expectations of cultural behavior are not explicit or communicated verbally. The rules are taken for granted; an outsider cannot enter easily because they do not have the internal context information. In low context societies, connections are of shorter duration and are often task oriented. Rules are external and knowledge of them is public. An airport or supermarket is an example; outsiders easily enter these low context situations because the environment contains the necessary information.

High and low context describe particular situations rather than a whole society, which contains both modes. High context culture develops in a stable population, not a highly mobile one.

TRANSMISSION OF HIGH CULTURE, FOLK CULTURE, AND POPULAR CULTURE

High culture is most often transmitted in written form and has a comparatively limited audience. For the deaf community, high culture transmitted in writing necessitates knowing another language. Much of folk culture is transmitted orally. Such things as marriage customs, stories, legends, and recipes are spread to an audience that is also limited, usually the community, family, or region. The deaf have full access to the traditions within the deaf community. Popular culture has a wide audience as it is transmitted through such far-reaching media as television, music, and the Internet. Though pop culture both reflects and shapes society while reinforcing its values, it is the least accessible for the deaf community. Communication technology and availability of interpreters level the field to some degree, but much of popular culture is still inaccessible to deaf people.

CULTURES, CONNECTIONS, COMPARISONS AND COMMUNITIES.

The cultures goal recognizes the importance of family, including meals, holidays, social events, friendship, greeting behaviors, and school practices. It examines the contributions of art and literature, significance of sports, movies, and television, as well as education. Connections examine health and physical education, sports and games, fine arts, the work of artists, and important historical events. The comparisons component examines the ways in which the language being learned uses features of the English language and vice versa. The communities goal identifies community events where the target language is used such as club meetings, festivals, or theater where contact may be made with native speakers.

COMMUNICATION IN VISUAL AND SPOKEN LANGUAGE

Hearing people tend to communicate quickly and efficiently; eye contact is not necessary for communication. Because spoken language users do not use their faces and bodies as freely as the Deaf, they may be perceived as stiff and emotionless. Facial expression and body language are integral to sign language; Deaf people read very subtle facial and body movements. More casual physical contact is expected in deaf culture, when greeting or leaving, to get attention, etc. In a spoken conversation, environmental noises take the attention of the speaker and often divert the speaker's eyes. In a signed conversation, eye contact is maintained at all times; lack of eye contact communicates indifference. Speaking directly to a deaf person, even when he is using an interpreter, is appropriate. Pointing is not considered rude, as it is in hearing culture. When there are deaf students in the classroom, it is important to take turns speaking and make sure the speaker can be identified.

INDIVIDUALISM

Most Americans think of themselves as separate individuals, responsible for their own lives. Americans place high importance on privacy - they value "personal space" and "personal thoughts." Many deaf people derive a sense of self from belonging to a community offering guidance and support. Members identify with their school, club, or perhaps a city with a large deaf population. In the deaf community, open communication is important. Withholding information or leaving a member to find out something on his own is not practiced in the Deaf community; the group is proud of the communication they have with each other. In Deaf culture, socializing is extremely important. In a society where the deaf make up a small minority and Deaf culture is commonly misunderstood, the support of others is especially valued.

INDIVIDUALISM AND COLLECTIVISM

While no society practices either individualism or collectivism exclusively, there are important differences. In an individualistic society, people are loosely connected; each person looks after himself. This is viewed as the dominant cultural pattern in the United States. Sayings such as "do your own thing" and "looking out for number one" are evidence of the separateness. Privacy holds an important place in this societal pattern - individuals defend their personal space and right to be alone.

In a collective society, the group acts together and people find their identity within the group. Membership in Deaf culture establishes social and behavioral norms. Once dependent on the community, it is believed that affluence, greater professional opportunity, and advances in communication technology are dividing the deaf community.

CULTURAL DETERMINISM, CULTURAL RELATIVISM, AND CULTURAL ETHNOCENTRISM

Cultural determinism takes the position that human nature is determined by values, beliefs, and meanings learned from one's society. Others' ideas are to be tolerated since people are conditioned to be the way they are. Cultural relativism understands that societies think and act differently. It does not imply that any one culture is intrinsically normal or inferior and tries to understand the reasons for cultural differences. Cultural ethnocentrism, on the other hand, believes its own culture is superior and that other ways of life are distorted. It expects its own ideas and methods to work everywhere.

TESTING CULTURAL ATTITUDES AND UNDERSTANDINGS

The Bogardus Social Distance Scale is designed to measure how closely a person is willing to participate with members of diverse racial, ethnic, or other social groups. The person taking the assessment rates his acceptance of someone from the other group in various scenarios: as a visitor to their country, a fellow citizen, co-worker, neighbor, close friend, or through marriage.

The Likert scale presents statements respondents rate as something they either strongly agree or strongly disagree with. The responses are tallied to show comparison or correlation of individual or group attitudes. The survey is used in sociology and psychology research.

The Guttman scale arranges preferences on a cumulative scale, rather than by intensity.

DEAF CULTURE WITH THAT OF OTHER ETHNIC GROUPS

Most ethnic and religious cultures have a distinct cuisine, special foods for feasts, dietary restrictions, staple foods, and traditional foods. Mode of dress identifies an ethnic or religious community, such as the Orthodox Jewish or Amish. Regional or historic costumes are a part of some cultures, such as western or Mexican. Many cultures share a common religion with attendant boundaries, ethics, and scriptural tradition. There is no specific deaf religion or church; no distinct geographical communities, food, or dress for the deaf. Instead, social customs, folklore and literary tradition, social and recreational institutions, schools, and a unique history are among the signifying aspects of Deaf culture. The overreaching mark of Deaf culture is its shared language: in the U.S.A., it is ASL.

Manifestation of cultural differences

The practices of a culture are revealed in symbols, heroes, rituals, and values.

- Symbols include both objects and words whose meaning is shared by members of a culture.
- Real, or fictional, heroes are models for the culture, exhibiting prized characteristics.
- Rituals such as greetings, demonstrations of respect, and religious ceremonies are essential to society.
- Values, what's thought to be right or wrong, natural or unnatural, cannot be observed; they are inferred through actions.

Culture exists on many levels: national, regional, generational, gender, corporate, and social class. Diversity in language, religion, education, and occupation may exist within the same culture.

Cultural differences are compared in a number of ways: the degree of inequality; to what extent uncertainty or ambiguity poses a threat; to what degree a society is individualistic or collective. Researchers have plotted certain values as relatively achievement or relationship dominant.

Using terms related to hearing

Deaf (capitalized) is the term used for members of the Deaf community, those who share a language, a history, similar values, and behaviors.

Deaf (not capitalized) is the term used for those hard of hearing or deafened and refers to the condition of being able to hear. Their primary language is English.

Hearing Impaired is the term used by society and the media to refer to people with hearing loss. It is an offensive phrase within the Deaf community, as it suggests something in need of repair.

Hearing is used within the Deaf culture to identify members of the dominant American culture, a designation for those who speak.

Maintaining cultural boundaries

ASL sets Deaf people apart as a group; the language is part of Deaf identity and strong attitudes are held concerning its use. Deaf people classify others by their language preference and may avoid a deaf person who uses signed English. Hearing people learning ASL as a second language may be viewed with suspicion. A Deaf person will often use an English form of signing when interacting with a hearing person, partly because the hearing person lacks ASL fluency and partly to maintain the integrity of the Deaf community. Variation in ASL is said to be sociolinguistic when attributed to factors such as education, race, age, sex, and geography. Variation can occur at phonological, syntactic, and lexical levels.

Medical, rehabilitation, legal, and social models of Deafness

A medical model of deafness sees deaf people as patients in need of treatment. The rehabilitation model sees the deaf as in need of assistive technology at home and on the job. The legal model views deaf people as citizens with the rights and responsibilities of every other citizen including accessibility to mass communication and the right to vote. A social model of deafness views deaf people not as in need of treatment, but as part of society's diversity with need for access. Technology in the medical model is prosthesis to affect a cure, or partial cure, such as hearing aids and cochlear implants. The rehabilitation model of deafness includes assistive technology as a means of help; access technology is needed in the legal model. Goals can be achieved through use of captioning, video- and text- telephones.

LANGUAGE PLANNING

Language planning is a government's policies concerning a language or languages. As society becomes increasingly multilingual, language differences call for legislation on language policies used in education and in access to services. The Court Interpreters Act, Voting Rights Act, and Bilingual Education Act are examples of such legislation.

In some countries, language planning results in the development or standardization of written form, expanded vocabulary, and syntactic development. Linguists, sociologists, and political scientists are involved in this assessment. Reduced language diversity is sometimes a result of language planning decisions. Educators respond to policies by developing programs; language academies may serve as arbiters in policy-making. The Center for Research and Documentation on World Language Problems publishes a multilingual journal, Language Problems and Language Planning.

DEAFHOOD VS. DEAFNESS

The term Deafhood is attributed to Paddy Ladd. Ladd's book, Understanding Deaf Culture: In Search of Deafhood has been called the "bible of deaf culture." Ladd calls Deafhood a process, "the struggle by each Deaf child, Deaf family and Deaf adult to explain to themselves and each other their own existence in the world." Deafhood is used to define the positive experience of being human, accepting oneself, using natural language, and validation by the group. Deafness describes a negative experience, defined by a medical condition that needs fixing. Deafhood resists audism, discrimination, and disparagement of sign language.

DEAF WAY

Deaf Way, its title taken from the sign that means "deaf way of life," took place in 1989 at Gallaudet University. Various estimates are given, but attendance was more than 5000 Deaf people who came from all over the world. They represented over eighty different signed languages. Deaf Way II in 2002 was reportedly attended by nearly 10,000 people from 120 countries. Billed as an educational conference and arts festival, it was held at the Washington Convention Center. The conferences were organized as a departure from the usual ones, which focus on the problems of being deaf. Planners wanted to present opportunities for ideas to be exchanged and accomplishments to be celebrated.

VALUE OF DIVERSITY TO THE DEAF CULTURE

Diversity is named as a core value of the National Association of the Deaf. The NAD seeks to build and maintain membership and foster leadership that reflects the diversity of the American Deaf community in terms of language, culture, race, gender, age, and socioeconomic status. Gallaudet University embraces diversity in its student body, faculty, learning, teaching, research, and service. It maintains an Office of Diversity and Equity for Students that advocates and empowers multicultural students to achieve success academically and personally. Its programs foster self-awareness, cultural growth, intellectual curiosity, academic support, and a stimulating learning environment. The Languagescape Vision of Texas School for the Deaf promotes the educational development of multilingual and multicultural students and supports positive attitudes towards diverse language uses within the community.

UNIVERSALITY OF DEAF CULTURE

No culture is entered by virtue of birth. Members must accept and share the values of a culture to become a member. While Deaf people throughout the world share the experience of living as a minority in a society where most people are hearing, Deaf culture is not the same across the globe. Deaf in America and Germany use different languages and their background histories are not the same. Being deaf does not grant membership into Deaf culture. Culture is not determined by possessions or objects (artifacts). Class status or level of education is not what determines membership in a culture. Religion, holidays, and music may reflect culture, but they are not what define it. Biological traits are not an indicator of culture.

DUAL HIERARCHY OF POWER

One model of hierarchy perceived within Deaf culture views hearing as the indicator of relative power, both economically and politically. White hearing men are most powerful; then white hearing women. Next in rank are minority hearing men and women, Deaf white men and women, with Deaf minority men and women at the bottom. When it comes to hearing, the hierarchy of power is reversed in the Deaf community. The deaf person who uses ASL, went to deaf school, and comes from a deaf family has the most power. Next in status is the ASL user who went to deaf school, but comes from a hearing family. Those who learned to sign later in life, became deaf at an early age, those deafened at a late age, and then hard of hearing each rank successively lower. A hearing person is at the bottom of the hierarchy.

EXPLORING CULTURE SYSTEMATICALLY

Using a cultural framework allows study of cultural details in context. A triangle model of product, practice, and perspective might be used thus:

When a product that is common to a number of cultures is being considered, practices and perspectives associated with the product are identified. Products don't have to be tangible; they can be language or literature. Perspectives could be from historical, political, social, religious, or family values and explore how they have changed. Any film, newspaper article, Website, or interaction with those in the target culture can be used to identify a product, practice, or perspective that can be related to the other aspects. Students reflect on the interrelationship of the three points. A journal can help students analyze their insights.

JAMES WOODWARD

Dr. James Woodward earned his PhD from Georgetown University in sociolinguistics and has held various positions at Gallaudet University for over twenty years. He has taught and done research in Hong Kong, Thailand, and Viet Nam. His published works include How You Gonna Get to Heaven If You Can't Talk With Jesus: On Depathologizing Deafness and Signs of Sexual Behavior. Woodward's research involves comparing sign languages, studying their history, and documenting endangered sign languages. He has identified seven sign languages used in Thailand and Vietnam, with modern Thai Sign being the only national language among them.

NAMES

Names are used differently in ASL than in English; in ASL, names are not used to get the person's attention. ASL users do not use name signs in greetings, as English speakers do. Instead of, "Hello, John," an ASL user simply signs "hello". Nor is a name sign used in conversation for emphasis, as in spoken English, such as, "John, did you see the game?" Name signs are used to refer to someone who is not present. A name sign is of great value to a Deaf person; it marks his membership in the Deaf community. It is not appropriate to ask a deaf person what his name sign means - English speakers don't ask each other "Why is your name John?"

DIFFICULTIES IN TEACHING CULTURE

Instructors can teach about culture. A teachers' responsibility is to stimulate interest in the culture, pointing out differences of and within the culture. They need to be careful not to corroborate prejudices, nor criticize students' convictions. They teach that no culture is superior to another. The foreign language classroom, multicultural in itself, provides opportunities for learning through interactions between participants.

Some teaching methods and educational policies widely used in the West may not be suited to other countries. The communicative approach to language teaching, for example, is global in nature. Minority languages could be lost where the goal is assimilation rather than bilingualism.

BAKER-SHENK AND COKELY'S MODEL OF DEAF CULTURE

Deaf culture involves four essential factors:

1. Audiological - the degree of hearing loss is less important than whether a person is perceived as DEAF or ORAL by other deaf people.
2. Social - how much a person associates with other Deaf people, by way of school, marriage, clubs, or events.
3. Political - whether a person has power in the Deaf community; a person who holds an office in a Deaf organization has political power.
4. Linguistic - most important of all is the use and support of American Sign Language.

The doctrine of cultural and linguistic relativity asserts that all cultures and languages have equal value. Spoken and signed languages are found in both highly civilized and less progressive societies. It is unscientific to read value comparisons into language evolution.

SOCIAL CHARACTERISTICS

Members of the deaf community are closely connected, a sense that is felt immediately when deaf people connect. Within the community is found a basis for political strength. A premium is placed on socialization and deaf people joke about DST, or Deaf Standard Time, because the tendency to keep talking often makes a person late. Sporting events and religious gatherings provide more opportunities to socialize. The degree of hearing loss does not figure largely in the deaf community; shared language is what counts. The percentage of deaf people that marry within the community is high, yet almost 90% of deaf children are born to hearing parents. Deaf is normal and deaf babies highly valued. Many deaf people identify themselves as Deaf before race or nationality.

PROFESSIONAL SIGN LANGUAGE INTERPRETER

An interpreter must have a thorough command of at least two languages. They facilitate communication between people without exerting personal influence. The interpreter transmits environmental sounds, as well as nonverbal expressions of humor and other nuances so that both participants have access to the same input. The physical position of the interpreter is important in terms of lighting, insufficient lighting can cause miscommunication; busy backgrounds in clothing and facial hair can also hinder communication. Interpreters work in a variety of settings, including schools, hospitals, government agencies, and other facilities. Interpreting is sometimes provided remotely.

Interpreting is governed by a code of ethics. Interpreters should not accept work for which they are not qualified. The Registry of Interpreters for the Deaf (RID), begun in 1964, establishes guidelines and evaluates interpreters.

DEAF COMMUNITY VS. HEARING COMMUNITY COMMUNICATION

Some aspects of Deaf interaction are unique.

Greeting - often involves touching to get a person's attention; waving, flashing lights, and stomping the floor are appropriate in some situations

Openness of communication - making information available to all; personal information is openly shared; being alert to environmental distractions such as poor lighting or visual interruptions; checks for comprehension are routinely made

Sharing information - affirms the unity of the community; because information is harder to come by, it is extremely valued. The value placed by hearing people on privacy, is hard for the Deaf community to understand, if not annoying.

Maintaining eye contact - turning ones back is an insult in deaf communication; lack of eye contact may signal disinterest

Leave-taking - explanations are given for the departure and arrangements to meet again are made; saying goodbye can take an hour

Aspects of American Deaf Culture

PUBLIC PERCEPTIONS

During the 1970's the Chair of Deaf Studies was established at Gallaudet University. Deaf men became superintendents at three state schools for the deaf and Texas passed a law recognizing ASL as a language. Deaf people protested when hearing actors took on deaf roles and shows like Sesame Street and Rainbow's End raised awareness and provided role models to deaf children. Lou Ferrigno, famous from his role as the Incredible Hulk, grew up with the nickname "Deaf Louie;" Ferrigno was chosen as Mr. America and Mr. Universe. A few news programs were developed for deaf audiences, closed captioning was being developed, and TTYs (teletypewriters) were coming into use. Warning lights were installed in the Washington, DC subway system. The first deaf jurors served. Deaf Awareness events were observed in many states, the National Center for Law and Deaf opened in 1975, and a legal defense fund was established. Interpreter laws were also passed, in order to facilitate communication.

DEAF PEOPLE VS. RACIAL, OR OTHER MINORITIES

Compared to immigrant groups, numbering in the millions and geographically clustered, deaf individuals composed a small portion of the population and were widely dispersed. Grouped with the mentally and physically disabled, deaf people were often rejected for employment. During the Depression, the Federal government classified the deaf as unemployable. 1920's licensing laws discriminated against deaf people, even though many worked at auto or tire factories; such laws led to further loss of employment. Insurance companies refused deaf clients. Labeled 'menace, defective, or dangerous,' the deaf lived with the threat of legislation to sterilize. Deaf people were often misdiagnosed as intellectually disabled or mentally ill, as intelligence testing was biased toward the hearing. While immigrants could gradually assimilate to the surrounding culture, the deaf always had to contend with the communication barrier.

At school, students faced an oppressive environment, separated from family and subject to excessive punishment. Schools were not identified as educational institutions, but rather asylums administered under welfare. The deaf were labeled disabled; they could not buy insurance nor obtain a driver's license, and were forced into menial jobs. The oralism movement saw deaf schools closed and deaf teachers replaced. As telephone, radio, and movies became more widely used, the deaf became increasingly isolated.

The National Fraternal Society of the Deaf, established in 1901, became the strongest organization of the deaf in America. The organization did not seek special legal protection for the deaf, nor did it want charity. The Society was a social outlet; it also offered insurance to deaf people. It supported a deaf labor bureau, calling for a federal bureau in 1934. The Society sponsored publicity campaigns and worked for equal rights as citizens.

ICED

The International Congress on the Education of the Deaf (ICED) is not an organization; it is an event held every five years, where educators and researchers meet to share information and ideas pertaining to the education of the deaf. The first conference was held in 1878 in Paris. In 2008, the Congress met for the 21st time in Vancouver, Canada. At this meeting, the Congress announced its formal rejection of resolutions passed in 1880 at the 2nd conference, held in Milan. The Congress in 1880 had voted in favor of the oral method of education, claiming it as superior to teaching

71

methods that use sign language. The next meeting of ICED, in 2015, will be held at the University of Patras, in Greece.

INTERNATIONAL SPORTS ORGANIZATION

104 national deaf sports federations belong to the Comité International des Sports des Sourds, CISS (The International Committee of Sports for the Deaf), formed in 1924. The first games organized for deaf athletes were held in Paris, France and were known as The Silent Games. 148 athletes from nine European nations took part. Now called the Summer and Winter Deaflympics, the games are sanctioned by the International Olympic Committee (IOC) and are one of the world's fastest growing sports events. At the 21st Summer Deaflympics in Taipei, over 2,000 athletes from over 75 countries competed. The games are distinctive, not only because of the special communication needs on the sports field, but for the element of social interaction in the games as well.

WFD

The World Federation of the Deaf is a central organization made up of national associations of Deaf people. 130 countries belong and represent about 70 million Deaf people. The National Association of the Deaf is the United States member.

Established in 1951, in Rome, Italy, WFD works to promote the human rights of Deaf people, notably the right to use sign language. WFD is a member of the International Disability Alliance and has consultative status in the United Nations. When necessary, WFD takes legal or administrative action to ensure that Deaf people in every country can preserve their sign languages and cultural activities. Areas of involvement for the WFD include better education for Deaf people, improved access to information and services, improved human rights for Deaf people in developing countries, improved status of national sign languages, and promoting the establishment of Deaf organizations.

INTERNATIONAL ORGANIZATIONS THAT SERVE THE DEAF

Global Deaf Connection (GDC) seeks to ensure that the deaf in developing countries have equal access to education and employment. GDC's vision is that Deaf people around the world gain access to universal human rights; the Deaf will gain economic self-sufficiency by actively using their native sign language; and Deaf communities will be sustained.

Deaf International (DI) is a non-profit organization dedicated to serving Deaf and Hard of Hearing communities around the world through education, advocacy, and opportunities for spiritual growth. DI helps develop literature for signed languages, increasing respect and recognition for these signed languages within the international community.

Deaf Pilots Association, with members in the US, Europe, and Australia, represents deaf pilots as they interact with organizations, such as the Federal Aviation Administration and the Aircraft Owners and Pilots Association. They maintain a library, website, publish a newsletter, and work to demonstrate the ability of deaf people to earn pilot certificates.

PATHOLOGICAL MODEL OF DEAFNESS WITH THE CULTURAL/LINGUISTIC VIEW

The pathological model of deafness seeks a cure and looks for ways to overcome the effects of deafness, which is viewed as a handicap. This philosophy emphasizes speech and views signing as inferior to spoken language. In this model, deafness is not accepted as a culture.

The culturally deaf model acknowledges deafness as a difference and values sign language, as it is the most natural language for the deaf. It finds its role models in successful deaf adults. It focuses on the subject matter, not the mode of communication in education. In the cultural model of deafness, vision is viewed as a positive alternative channel to efficient communication. It does not deny deafness; rather, it values socialization within the deaf community and works for access to the same rights and privileges enjoyed by hearing people.

EDUCATION OF AMERICAN DEAF CHILDREN PRIOR TO 1817

The deaf, before the 16th century, were widely considered to be uneducable. Few believed they were capable of having ideas or reasoning; Aristotle had taught that the deaf could not be educated. Lacking language, they were treated as not fully human. With the lack of expectation that they could learn, deaf children were often neglected, treated with indifference, or kept in a state of dependence. Some children were kept in a room or allowed to wander the streets. Along with children who were blind or otherwise physically disabled, if deaf children were educated at all, it was through private tutoring. Otherwise, they lived and worked within the family, using gestures or home signs to communicate. If the family had means, a child might be sent to Europe, where schools for the deaf had already been established.

19TH CENTURY SCHOOLS FOR THE DEAF

Schools for the deaf in the 1800's were more than educational facilities; they took on the responsibility of feeding, housing, and instilling proper conduct in their students. The schools included sleeping quarters, dining halls, and classrooms. Parents or guardians relinquished control of their deaf child to the institution; children were away from their homes and families for long periods. The environment was often oppressive, with strict rules and easily earned punishment. Imbalance of power was experienced, not only in relation to staff, but also in a hierarchy among students. A high degree of separation from the hearing community was enforced, as was a division of the sexes. Iron fences and gates were typical on deaf school campuses. Students coming to the residential schools from isolated environments that made them constantly aware of their deafness discovered there were others who couldn't hear; they were not as unique as they had believed.

DEAF PRESIDENT NOW PROTEST OF 1988

Because of the so-called rubella-bulge, there were more deaf young adults in the nation than at any other time when the president of Gallaudet University announced his resignation in 1988. Two of the three candidates being considered to replace him were deaf, but Elisabeth Zinser, who did not know ASL, was chosen. Students protested, asking for a Deaf president and a majority of Deaf board members. Staff, faculty, and alumni joined in a peaceful demonstration that lasted a week. The events were nationally publicized. I. King Jordan was subsequently appointed as the first deaf president of Gallaudet, serving almost twenty years. Deaf President Now (DPN) is considered a watershed event in the empowerment of deaf people.

TOTAL COMMUNICATION

Total Communication (TC), rather than a specific instructional method or course of study, refers to a philosophy that promotes free and unrestricted communication. It combines oral, manual, and auditory modes, eliminating the need to choose between a strictly oral or manual communication method. Signs are used simultaneously with speech so that each reinforces the other. Gestures, signs, speech, fingerspelling, reading, and writing are included so that a child can learn according to his own needs and capabilities. Residual hearing is developed and speechreading skills enhanced through amplification. Roy Holcomb coined the term in 1967. TC was developed at the Maryland School for the Deaf. During the 1970's and 1980's, the TC philosophy was the most common philosophy used in educating deaf children.

LAURENT CLERC

Clerc was a teacher and former student at the National School for the Deaf, in Paris. When Thomas Gallaudet visited the school to learn its methods, Clerc agreed to come to America, where he would

73

help organize the first deaf school at Hartford, CT. On the voyage, Clerc taught Gallaudet sign language, while he learned English himself. With Gallaudet, Clerc toured the northeastern United States, gaining support for the school and others that would soon follow it. Clerc was head teacher at Hartford school for 41 years. He asked for, and gained, federal support from Congress for the school. Besides his ability as a teacher, Clerc set an example: because of his success using sign language to educate the deaf in Paris, sign language was the norm in the first United States schools for the deaf.

ORAL MOVEMENT OF THE EARLY 20TH CENTURY

Sign language, it was thought, prevented deaf students from learning to speak English. Educational reformers campaigned to eliminate the use of sign language in the classroom in favor of *oralism*. The goal was to teach the deaf to speak through a method of painstaking and uncomfortable therapy. The method made exclusive use of lipreading and speech. Oralists, notably Alexander Graham Bell, charged that sign language set deaf people apart; he thought deaf shouldn't marry each other and produce more deaf children.

By 1920, 80 percent of deaf students were taught orally and the number of deaf teachers declined. Most deaf students continued to use sign language outside the classroom, even though they were forbidden to use it in school.

Men and women who were deaf have played an important role in deaf education

The success of the first public school for the deaf in Paris was due to the involvement of deaf persons. Speakers of native sign language informed the method of instruction. L'Epee valued sign language and believed the deaf possessed normal intelligence. He didn't try to make his students oral; his method was to have deaf students go on to teach other deaf students. One such student was Laurent Clerc who functioned fully using sign language, and expected students to put forth their best efforts. Jean Massieu, born deaf, instructed Laurent Clerc in Paris and went on to start another school for the deaf in France. Edward Miner Gallaudet's deaf mother was matron of the school her son founded in Washington.

TEXAS DEPARTMENT OF ASSISTIVE AND REHABILITATIVE SERVICES

The Texas Department of Assistive and Rehabilitative Services (DARS) is an agency that oversees programs of early intervention, vocational rehabilitation, and independent living opportunities for Texans with disabilities. Its goals are to improve the quality of the lives of the disabled and enable them to pursue independent and productive lives. DARS combines the operations of four divisions that formerly provided separate services for Blind, Rehabilitation, Early Childhood, and Disability Determination Services.

Located in Austin, specialists located across the state can provide hearing loss information and advocacy. Through DARS, deaf students can apply for tuition waver and access The Specialized Telecommunication Assistance Program (STAP) a voucher program that assists with the purchase of telephone equipment. The agency provides information and publications on interpreter services and training, hearing aids, and telecommunications devices.

2ND INTERNATIONAL CONGRESS FOR EDUCATORS OF THE DEAF

Resolutions passed by the convention acknowledged the "incontestable superiority of articulation over signs" and therefore the oral method should be used in education and instruction of the deaf. The pure oral method was recommended over the combined method, which used both signs and speech. Pupils receiving oral instruction should be in classes separate from those who had previously been taught in sign. Implementation of the resolutions caused sign language to be suppressed and many deaf teachers were replaced with those who can hear.

Of the 164 participants in the conference, five were Americans who represented fifty-one schools and more than 6,000 students, more than the other delegates combined. Though they proposed compromises, American educators were outvoted ten to one.

NATIONAL ASSOCIATION FOR THE DEAF

The National Association for the Deaf (NAD), established in 1880, is a civil rights organization for Deaf and Hard of Hearing. NAD has associations in every state and represents the United States in the World Federation of the Deaf. One of NAD's goals is to preserve and foster respect for American Sign Language. To learn and use ASL is viewed as an essential human right. Diversity and inclusiveness are embraced as foundational values in the NAD.

Areas of involvement include early intervention, education, employment, health care, legal justice, and technology. Youth leadership programs include summer camps where deaf and hard of hearing high school students have the opportunity to develop scholarship, leadership, and citizenship. Biennial NAD Conferences are held in the even numbered years.

DOGS FOR THE DEAF PROGRAM

Founded in 1977 by Hollywood animal trainer Roy G. Kabat, Dogs for the Deaf chooses dogs between eight months and three years old from shelters in the northwest and California. The dogs chosen have important traits such as friendliness and confidence. The dogs receive extensive obedience and socialization training for a period of four to six months, and are trained using positive reinforcement. Hearing Dogs respond to sounds in the home—smoke alarm, telephone, door knock or doorbell, alarm clock, and timer. The dogs alert a deaf person when his or her name is called or when their baby cries. The dog can be taught to alert their owner to any repetitive sound, such as the microwave or teakettle. In public, a Hearing Dog makes the person more aware of his or her environment, as it reacts to sounds it hears. Over 3,000 dogs have been trained and placed; qualified applicants are not charged for the service.

COMMUNICATION ACCESS REALTIME TRANSLATION (CART)

A method of translating speech to text, Communication Access Realtime Translation or Computer Aided Real–Time Captioning is real-time captioning that can be delivered on location or remotely. Using a stenographic machine and laptop computer, the CART specialist transcribes every word and projects the captions onto a screen or an individual's computer monitor; it can even be integrated with a video presentation as captions. The display, such as closed captioning, provides identification of the speaker as well as a description of environmental sounds. The quickly growing service is gaining acceptance in schools and the workplace. Because the transcription is in real time, a deaf person can actively participate in classes or conferences. In addition, a text copy is created.

CLOSED CAPTIONING

Closed captions are electronic codes that supply and display a written transcript to television broadcasts, videotapes, and DVD's. Closed captioning provides text for not only the dialogue and narration, but it also gives a description of sounds, such as a laugh or slamming door. Coming into use in the 1980's, closed captions required a decoder; a built-in decoder chip was developed in the early 1990's. Unlike subtitled movies, closed captioning can be turned on or off; white letters on a black background are placed either above or below the picture. Pre-recorded programming has fewer mistakes in captioning; in real-time captioning, where there is no time to proofread or correct errors, computers assist with supplying names and geographic locations. Closed captioned video is identified by the symbol CC.

In 1976, the Federal Communications Commission designated line 21 of television transmissions to be used exclusively for closed captions. In 1979, HEW created the National Captioning Institute. Congress passed the Americans with Disabilities Act (ADA) in 1990, which states that businesses and public accommodations must not discriminate against individuals with disabilities. Title III of the ADA expressly called for public facilities, including hospitals and museums, to provide access to verbal information. Also in1990, the Television Decoder Circuitry Act mandated that television sets more than 13" wide must include caption-decoding technology. In1996, the Telecommunications Act set forth rules and deadlines for the captioning of television programming. In 1998 Section 508 of the Rehabilitation Act of 1973 was amended by Congress to eliminate barriers in information technology. On October 8, 2010, the Twenty-First Century Communications and Video Accessibility Act became law.

TELEPHONE

The invention and subsequent widespread use of the telephone has changed the way the world communicates. Without having to know Morse code, anyone could connect with family and friends or do business. Anyone, that is, except deaf people. Telephone use required in employment excluded deaf people from certain jobs. There wasn't a way for a deaf person to contact emergency services; deaf people relied on their neighbors or children to make calls for them, or drove to see the person they needed to converse with.

After the development of the TTY, deaf people could communicate over distances. It was made possible for the Deaf to take action as a community, working together for equal access to communication. TTYs made it possible for deaf people to contact businesses and government agencies.

Deaf physicist Robert Weitbrecht invented the acoustic coupler modem in 1964. Early TTYs were expensive; they consisted of a teletype machine, an acoustic coupler, and a telephone set and, at first, could be used for only one-way communication. In 1968, less than 200 TTYs were in use; by 1982, 180,000 were in use. In 1973 the first electronic portable TDD (Telephone Device for the Deaf) was developed and cost $599. The TDD used five-bit Baudot code, incompatible with the ASCII code used by computers. The term "TDD" is most often used by those outside the deaf community, which prefers the term "TTY."

TTY users type GA for "Go Ahead" to signal the end of speaking. SK = "Stop Keying,"

SKSK means "Now hanging up." Using a TTY, calls can be placed to a Telecommunications Relay Service, through which it is possible for the deaf to call regular phone users.

INVENTIONS

Advances in mass communication were thrilling developments for hearing people. Silent movies could be enjoyed by all, but the "talkies" were inaccessible to the deaf. The advent of radio made news, weather, and other programming available to all who could hear. The telephone, for nearly a century, was a barrier, instead of an asset, to communication for the deaf.

The development of TTY and relay services helped level the playing field. Devices like flashers, to signal the doorbell or ringing of the telephone, were also helpful. Much smaller hearing aids and FM systems were developed and cochlear implants came into wider use. Dramatic improvement in data processing power, digitization and miniaturization, explosion of the Internet and email, and use of mobile phones, together with new public policies, have revolutionized communication for the deaf.

NAME SIGNS

A Deaf person places great value on his name sign. Possession of a name sign shows membership in the Deaf community. Although a Deaf person has an English name on his birth certificate, a name sign serves as a symbol for his identity and makes socialization possible. Fingerspelling of names sometimes occurs in the Deaf community, but name signs function more effectively. Name signs can show family or group relationships and relative importance or power within the community. Siblings' name signs often share the same location.

A person's name sign represents his identity throughout life. It is changed only if another person has the same sign, in which case the newcomer or younger person modifies his name sign, usually by adding an additional handshape. Hearing persons did not, historically, have name signs.

Arbitrary Name Signs (ANS) do not have inherent meaning. They combine a small set of hand shapes with certain possible locations and movements, using ASL rules. ANS is an alphabetic representation of the first, middle, or last name. A true name sign avoids certain locations, like the mouth, and should not be an actual sign, like 'police'. It uses neutral signing space and a single location on the body which is repeated, or dual locations on the body. Traditional, adult name signs are arbitrary.

Descriptive Name Signs (DNS) incorporate personal or physical features. Often invented by children for each other, DNSs will not carry into adulthood. The distinction is becoming blurred as nontraditional name signs are introduced by inexperienced signers and deaf children are increasingly given nontraditional name signs by hearing parents. Non-traditional name signs are acceptable if intended for amusement.

FACE-TO-FACE INTERACTION

Deaf culture focuses on visual stimulation. Video logs (vlogs) are one way Deaf people communicate; similar to blogs, they allow the Deaf to communicate in their primary language. Carnivals are another important mode of transmitting culture; at these large gatherings of Deaf people from across the country, storytelling and other forms of Deaf performance art are made possible. ASL literature is shared by poets, comedians, and other performers. New works are often created at fairs and large conventions of the Deaf. Here the community celebrates the freedom to share their language and culture apart from the majority culture; they experience a sense of connection and shared understanding of what it means to be deaf.

BLACK DEAF COMMUNITY

The Black Deaf community has features in common with the Deaf community, most notably in regard to communication. Blacks have been stereotyped in the same way as the Deaf: as dumb or handicapped. The Black Deaf community also has features in common with the Black community, such as facing societal prejudice, high unemployment, and lack of political leadership. They share in Black heritage. Shared language is important to socialization in both groups.

Unique to the Black Deaf community, however, are the clubs that, in many cities, are separate from White Deaf clubs. School segregation resulted in less educational opportunities. A Black Deaf individual is likely to marry a member of that same community. Fewer Deaf Black people have access to telecommunication devices. Differences in black and white signing also testify to the existence of a Deaf Black community. Some members identify themselves as Black, then Deaf.

CONVERSATIONAL MANNERISMS

Deaf communication is more direct and less inhibited than spoken communication. Facial expression and body movement are integral to American Sign Language. Facial expressions in hearing cultures are limited in contrast. One facial feature that is constrained in ASL is exaggerated mouth movements; only certain mouth movements are used. Eye contact is essential to communication in deaf community. In hearing culture, protracted eye contact would be considered staring. When a deaf person intends to leave the room, he tells others, even if it's just to go to the restroom, so others know why he has disappeared. Unlike among hearing diners, a waiter may touch a diner's shoulder to get his attention. A deaf person is not considered rude for walking between people having a conversation.

UNIFYING ASPECTS

Essential to identifying with Deaf culture is the use of American Sign Language. Fluency in ASL is not the only indicator of Deaf identity: group loyalty and shared history are also part of Deaf identity, something that hearing persons, including fluent signers, cannot fully acquire. The Deaf community is proud of its ability to overcome adversity and enjoys a sense of well-being and belonging. Deaf couples desire to pass on the language and values of their culture to deaf children. Deaf also have the experience of using assistive devices in common, usually signaling a ringing telephone or doorbell or alert that the baby is crying. They oppose a pathological view of deafness, instead regarding themselves as a linguistic/cultural minority. Deaf share the experience of interacting with hearing people - the challenge of trying to communicate successfully without benefit of sign language.

DEAF COMMUNITY IN RUSSIA

Much of what is known about Deaf culture in Western Europe and America focuses on educational experience and shared sign language. Social identity for the Deaf in Russia was established by other factors. Unlike deaf education in Western nations, which began as the work of Christians, education of deaf Russians was established by secular means. Sign language was recognized by the Tsars and schools for the Deaf were established in cities. Because educational infrastructure in Russia was weak, oralism didn't predominate as it did in the West. Deaf teachers kept sign language in the classroom. Deaf people were benefited by the All-Russian Organization for the Deaf (VOG) which created Rabfaks, where only deaf workers were employed. These enclosed facilities became enclaves of Deaf culture; in them, Deaf values were the norm. The state funded deaf sports and art exhibits. Mime troupes were well received by public audiences in Russia.

NTID

The Performing Arts department of the National Technical Institutes of the Deaf (NTID) in Rochester, New York was established in 1974 by Dr. Robert Panara. The first deaf person on the faculty at Rochester Institute of Technology (of which NTID is part), Panara was founder and director of NTID's Experimental Educational Theatre. The program offers a theatre course, including acting, technical theatre, and dance. Each NTID Performing Arts production is performed in ASL and spoken English at the same time, making it accessible to both deaf and hearing audience members.

Most Deaf theatre professionals have been either students or faculty at NTID. They have appeared in motion pictures, television, Broadway and international theatre tours.

DEAF THEATER

In deaf theater, each character has two actors who perform simultaneously: deaf actors sign while hearing actors speak. Among the challenges of producing deaf theatre is translating the script into

Sign Language - it must be both linguistically and culturally correct. Background scenery and costume design has to be adapted for ease of reading signs, yet without distorting historical accuracy. Ways to visually represent off-stage dialog, accents, jokes, and sound effects must be devised. Sightlines must be maintained so that audience and actors can see the signed dialog at all times. In place of headsets, video cameras and televisions are placed backstage and in dressing rooms; as such, cues must be made visually. For safety's sake, signs, lights, and glow tape are used.

DEAF HUMOR

Humor is an important part of deaf culture. It is suggested that deaf humor is a way of dealing with the oppression experienced by a minority group. Pros and cons of deafness are often portrayed humorously. In traditional deaf jokes and stories, the deaf person comes out the winner because he or she is deaf. Some deaf humor is linguistic; the way signs are produced or misproduced is what makes the audience laugh. Other humor employs an inappropriate register of communication. Visual puns are another example of deaf jokes. Taste in humor is subjective, just as among hearing people. There have been well-known deaf comedians.

STORYTELLING

Before the advent of video, and other technology, communication for Deaf people meant coming face to face with each other. Storytelling is a traditional means by which the Deaf community passes down the history and wisdom of the culture. Because most Deaf do not have Deaf parents, the Deaf community hands down the stories.

Deaf storytelling differs from hearing story telling in that it is not linear. It interweaves scenes, repeats for emphasis, and uses questions to create dialog. The emphasis in deaf storytelling is on the performance. Using facial expressions, gestures, and their bodies, ASL storytellers bring their stories to life. Storytelling using ASL has been shown to improve deaf students' reading, writing, and comprehension abilities.

A fundamental part of Deaf culture, ASL stories include legends, personal experiences, and fables. Skilled storytellers and poets are respected for their skill in the use of ASL. "Birds of a Different Feather" by Ben Bahan is a well-known fable. Artistic forms of ASL are structured differently than in ordinary communication. A-to-Z stories, also called ABC stories, date back to the 19th century and have been passed down from generation to generation. In these stories, each sign represents a letter of the manual alphabet and is difficult to translate because of the added visual effects. Numerical stories are similar, but told with numbers. Humorous stories are popular. One classic story portrays the storyteller's head as a golf ball; visual images communicate what happens before and after it is hit. In percussion signing, a drum or other instrument keeps a rhythm to which the performer signs. Its origin is at Gallaudet University football games in the 1940's.

ASL POETRY

It is likely that much deaf poetry created before the era of video recording devices has been lost, since it is visual, not written, and sign language has been suppressed. The same features in spoken language poetry can be identified in ASL poetry. In ASL poetry, signing is more flexible, with signs chosen for their physical form as a way of producing rhyme, meter, and rhythm. Several types of rhyme are used: movement path rhyme, NMS (nonmanual signal) rhyme, location rhyme, handedness rhyme, and end rhyme. Meter depends on visual movement. Poets frequently invent new signs to communicate their art. Ella Mae Lentz, Clayton Valli, and Patrick Graybill are well known for their ASL poetry.

GEORGE M. TEEGARDEN AND LOUIS FRISINO

George Teegarden attended Iowa School for the Deaf and graduated from Gallaudet. Teegarden was the first teacher at the Western Pennsylvania School for the Deaf, where he taught for 48 years, started the printing department and the school's magazine. He reported for The Pittsburgh News and the Deaf-Mute's Journal. Teegarden wrote and published books, stories, and poetry including "The Raindrop" using the pseudonym T.G. Arden.

Louis Frisino, deaf from birth, graduated from the Maryland School for the Deaf and Maryland Institute College of Art. His awards include the Peabody Award. A commercial artist with the News American, Frisino specializes in wildlife art.

JOHN CARLIN

Artist and poet John Carlin, born in Philadelphia in 1813 to an impoverished family, was profoundly deaf from infancy. He was one of the first students at the Pennsylvania School for the Deaf. At age twelve, Carlin supported himself by painting signs and houses. At twenty-five he traveled to Europe and studied under Delaroche. Upon returning to the United States, Carlin worked as a portrait artist, specializing in miniatures on ivory, which he sold to New York's prominent families. The Kentucky School for the Deaf commissioned Carlin to do a portrait of Laurent Clerc.

Carlin also published verses including "The Deaf-Mutes Lament," scientific articles for the Saturday Post, and a children's book. Even though he had only four years of formal schooling, Carlin's success helped advance education for the deaf.

LINDA BOVE

From 1971 to 2003, the deaf actress, Linda Bove, portrayed Linda the Librarian on the children's television program Sesame Street. On the program, she taught American Sign Language, introducing it to millions of kids and their parents. At the same time, she provided a positive role model to deaf children. Appearances on the TV shows Search for Tomorrow and Happy Days brought her in front of other large television audiences.

A graduate of Gallaudet University, Linda joined the National Theater for the Deaf. After the theater company did some work for Sesame Street, the Linda the Librarian character was created for her. This performance is distinguished as the longest role in the entertainment industry played by a Deaf person. With her husband, Linda founded Deaf West Theater, which stages plays and musical productions performed simultaneously in ASL and spoken English. Linda has published a number of books designed to teach ASL to children.

DEAF MEN IN BASEBALL

A plaque in the National Baseball Hall of Fame credits an umpire named Bill Klem with inventing the signs used in baseball. Others attribute them to William Ellsworth "Dummy" Hoy, a baseball player from the late 1800's. Hoy does get credit for hitting the first grand slam in the majors; he ranks in the top twenty-five on the list of stolen bases. Hoy, perhaps the most famous deaf athlete, opened the way for other deaf athletes to enter professional baseball. Luther Taylor pitched for the New York Giants, helping the team win pennants in 1904 and 1905 and the World Series in 1905. Edward Dundon played for the Atlanta Braves and is thought to be the first professional deaf umpire. Curtis Pride, major league outfielder and designated hitter, retired from professional baseball in 2008. Pride now coaches a university baseball team - Gallaudet.

LEGISLATION THAT AFFECTS THE EDUCATION OF DEAF CHILDREN

Section 504 of the Rehabilitation Act of 1973 made it illegal for individuals to be excluded, denied benefits, or be discriminated against because of a disability from programs or activities that receive Federal funding. The Education of All Handicapped Children Act (Public Law 94-142), enacted in 1975, required that students with disabilities be provided with accommodations and free appropriate public education in the least restrictive environment up to the age of 21. Amendments were added in 1986 pertaining to Education of the Handicapped. The Individuals with Disabilities Education Act (IDEA), which encompasses all laws pertaining to equal public education for children with disabilities, was enacted in 1990. In 2002, No Child Left Behind (NCLB) was authorized. It requires that Deaf and hard of hearing students be educated using the same standards-based curriculum that applies to their peers.

IDEA AND SECTION 504 OF THE REHABILITATION ACT

Under the Individuals with Disabilities Education Act (IDEA), a student qualifies for services based on a full comprehensive evaluation and the recommendation of a multidisciplinary team, which determines whether special instruction is needed. An Individualized Education Program (IEP) is written. It requires signed consent and IEP meetings must be attended by certain designated participants. Related services and modifications must be provided. IDEA is enforced by the Department of Education and the Office of Special Education Programs.

Section 504 of the Rehabilitation Act requires that services be provided to a student for whom a physical or mental impairment limits a major life activity. Educational performance need not be adversely affected to make the student eligible. Rather than a written IEP document, under Section 504, a plan is made to provide education comparable to that of non-handicapped students. Related services, building, and program accessibility are required. This law is enforced by the U.S. Office of Civil Rights.

FOUR PARTS OF ADA

The ADA is comprised of four parts:

1. Title 1 regards employment and prohibits exclusion from hiring based solely on disability. Reasonable effort must be made to accommodate individuals with disability needs.
2. Title 2 addresses access for individuals with disabilities to public transportation as well as state and local government properties, programs, and services.
3. Title 3 concerns public accommodations offered by businesses and non-profit organizations including restaurants, hotels, doctors' offices, recreation facilities, and day care centers. Individuals with disabilities may not be excluded, separated, or discriminated against. The law calls for the removal of architectural barriers where feasible.
4. Title 4 requires access to communication and media through services such as closed captioning. 24-hour relay services must be provided by telephone companies.

PROTECTING THE EDUCATIONAL RIGHTS OF CHILDREN WITH DISABILITIES

The Individualized Education Program (IEP) requires schools to develop a plan to address the student's need, regardless of what type or how severe the disability is. Appropriate aids and services must be provided, which may include interpreters for students who are deaf. Decisions about placement may not be made based on presumption or stereotype of a class of persons. Procedures for evaluation and placement prohibit unnecessary labeling, misclassification, or incorrect placement. The school district conducts or arranges for evaluation prior to placement, or before a major change in placement is implemented. Parents have the right to challenge such placement under due process. An Office for Civil Rights (OCR), headquartered in Washington, D.C., is maintained to enforce Section 504 and other civil rights laws.

Work written and performed by Deaf artists

Through art, students begin to understand the richness and fullness of the lives of Deaf people. Works by Deaf poets written as long ago as the sixteenth century, along with works by contemporary playwrights and actors, can instill a sense of the Deaf culture in a person. Names like Robert Panara, Gilbert Eastman, Bernard Bragg, Dorothy Miles, Ella Mae Lentz, and Robert Smithdas should be recognized as important deaf artists. Ben Bahan's essays are humorous and a good way for hearing students to get a sense of Deaf identity and the cultural power struggle. Deaf Heritage: A Narrative History of Deaf America by Jack Gannon is an excellent source of Deaf history, culture, and poetry. When the Mind Hears: A History of the Deaf by Harlan Lane is another classic.

TExES Practice Test

1. Basic Interpersonal Communication Skills (BICS)

a. are cognitively demanding
b. include new ideas and words
c. are used in informal social talk
d. apply to use in novel situations

2. According to Cummins' Additive Model of language acquisition, which is correct?

a. Experience with a second language does not promote first-language proficiency
b. Experience with the first language does not promote second-language proficiency
c. Experience with either the first or second language promotes proficiency in both
d. Experience with the first language only promotes proficiency in a second language

3. The SUP approach to language acquisition proposes that

a. learning the first language facilitates learning a second
b. acquisitions of first and second language are unrelated
c. learning a second language improves the first language
d. acquisitions of first and second languages have synergy

4. In language acquisition theory, which is true about the "affective filter"?

a. Having a high affective filter promotes the best learning
b. Having a low affective filter facilitates optimum learning
c. Having an affective filter distorts the meanings of words
d. Having an affective filter promotes social language uses

5. In the PEPSI model of language development, the first "P" stands for which of the below?

a. Pre-production
b. Productive use
c. Proficient usage
d. Prior to fluency

6. In the PEPSI model of language development, the "EP" stands for "Early Production." This stage is characterized by which of the following?

a. One- or two-word phrases
b. Use of simple sentences
c. Using complex sentences
d. Excellent comprehension

7. In the PEPSI model of language development, what does the "S" stand for?

a. Silent
b. Short
c. Simple
d. Speech

8. In the PEPSI model of language development, what does the final "I" represent?

a. Individual
b. Intelligent
c. Independent
d. Intermediate

9. The concept of "Input + 1" refers to which answer below?

a. Input slightly above the learner's level
b. Input from one speaker plus one more
c. Input via speech plus one more medium
d. Input, plus one additional linguistic factor

10. Which theorist posited the existence of an innate Language Acquisition Device?

a. Krashen
b. Terrell
c. Chomsky
d. Galyean

11. Normally developing babies will stop crying, turn to the speaker, and smile at familiar voices, stop activity and attend to unfamiliar voices, and respond to familiar or unfamiliar vocal tones at which age?

a. At birth
b. 0-3 months
c. 4-6 months
d. 7-12 months

12. At which age should you expect a normally developing child to understand two-step instructions?

a. 7-12 months
b. 3-4 years
c. 1-2 years
d. 5-6 years

13. Your 3-month-old baby smiles, coos, and cries differently to express hunger or pain, but does not babble. Your baby is which of the below?

a. Developmentally normal
b. Developmentally delayed
c. Developmentally disabled
d. Developmentally advanced

14. Your child often uses expressions like "Watch this!", "Heavy!", and "Mommy here?" This child is most likely between what ages?

a. 7 and 12 months
b. 1 and 2 years
c. 2 and 3 years
d. 3 and 4 years

15. Historically, who was the first to propose that Deaf people could learn language via signs?
   a. Spaniard Juan Pablo de Bonet (in 1620)
   b. Spanish Pedro Ponce de Leon (1520-84)
   c. Ancient Greek Aristotle (384-322 BC)
   d. Italian Geronimo Cardano (1501-1575)

16. Who founded the world's first school for the Deaf?
   a. Abbé de L'Epée in France
   b. Samuel Heinicke in Germany
   c. Thomas Hopkins Gallaudet in the United States of America
   d. Laurent Clerc in the United States of America

17. Which of the following sports-related developments was influenced by deaf athletes?
   a. Baseball umpires' hand signals
   b. Football teams forming huddles
   c. Gestuno, now International Sign
   d. All were caused by deaf players

18. Current research finds that babies can learn sign language
   a. much earlier than they can learn spoken language
   b. at the same ages that they learn spoken language
   c. much later than they could learn spoken language
   d. but this will not affect their spoken language development

19. According to research, which is true about deaf children and American Sign Language (ASL)?
   a. Children must be taught correct grammar to use ASL with meaning
   b. Children never develop anything like ASL without direct instruction
   c. Children demonstrate inherent ability to generate grammar in ASL
   d. Children who learn manually encoded English have difficulty in ASL

20. Research has found that abilities to generate, maintain, and transform visual and visual-spatial images are best in which of the following?
   a. Only hearing people who do not know or use any ASL
   b. Only hearing people who are fluent in the use of ASL
   c. Only deaf people who communicate by the use of ASL
   d. Hearing and deaf people who are both fluent with ASL

21. Which of the following is most accurate regarding sign languages for the deaf?
   a. American Sign Language is more like British Sign Language than like French Sign Language
   b. American Sign Language is significantly different from British and French Sign Languages
   c. American Sign Language is equally like French Sign Language as it is like British Sign Language
   d. American Sign Language is mutually understandable with British and French Sign Language

22. Immersion methods for learning a second language are most similar to which of the below?

    a. Submersion methods
    b. One-way methods
    c. Two-way methods
    d. Direct methods

23. A native French speaker visiting America says, "I hope my change of plan did not derange you." An American listener wonders why she thinks a plan change would make one crazy (deranged). What is this an example of?

    a. Interference
    b. Interlanguage
    c. Fossilization
    d. A and B only

24. Regarding the interrelations of culture and language, which statement is most correct?

    a. Passing social traditions to new generations typically relies upon written language
    b. A community's language usually reflects its most significant ideas and interactions
    c. Sharing the same language means community residents have similar moral beliefs
    d. Linguistic structures are preserved intact through a community's cultural traditions

25. Deaf culture is typically transmitted to succeeding generations by which idea below?

    a. Communications among members of deaf families
    b. Saving and handing down photos and other visuals
    c. Maintaining and passing down written documents
    d. Communications among members of communities

26. The Cognitive Academic Language Learning Approach (CALLA) divides learning strategies into three categories. Which is NOT one of these three?

    a. Cognitive
    b. Academic
    c. Metacognitive
    d. Social-Affective

27. Which is correct about a Home Language Survey giving information on a student's language background?

    a. This form is typically completed by a school social worker
    b. This form is typically completed by a language arts teacher
    c. This form is typically completed by the student's parents
    d. This form is typically completed optionally for all students

28. Of the following, whose theory most emphasizes social interaction ("nurture") in second language acquisition more than innate mechanisms ("nature")?

    a. Vygotsky
    b. Chomsky
    c. Krashen
    d. Terrell

29. Which of these is a similarity rather than a difference between what Deaf culture and hearing cultures find important?

    a. People having achieved a mastery of ASL
    b. People having excellent storytelling skills
    c. Parents' instilling values in their children
    d. Thinking and speaking as hearing people

30. What statement is most accurate regarding schools for the deaf versus mainstream education?

    a. Residential schools are irrelevant to transmission of Deaf culture
    b. Socialization enabling growth is facilitated by a common language
    c. Deaf residential students have more limited access to role models
    d. Deaf schools offer fewer opportunities to participate in activities

31. Which of the following is true about the Direct Method and Direct Experience Method (DEM) for teaching a second language including ASL?

    a. ASL is taught through using equal amounts of the native language and second language
    b. Grammar and pronunciation are less important than comprehension and communication
    c. DEM teaches both receptive and expressive skills and concrete and abstract vocabulary
    d. Teacher-student call-and-response interactions and rote repetition reflect DEM's design

32. Which statement is correct regarding Krashen and Terrell's Natural Approach to learning a second language including ASL?

    a. Students should be alert and vigilant, not relaxed, for the optimal learning
    b. Conversations, radio, and other everyday communications are important
    c. It is important to analyze a language first to understand it in this approach
    d. Students should be encouraged to use language even if they feel unready

33. In the Notional-Functional approach to teaching second languages including ASL, which is true?

    a. General notions are used to express thoughts, ideas, and feelings
    b. General notions equate to contexts or situations such as education
    c. Specific notions include such things as quantity, quality, and space
    d. Specific notions are unrelated to things like names and addresses

34. In the Notional-Functional approach to teaching second languages including ASL, what is correct about functions?

    a. The authors of this teaching approach identified seven functions of language
    b. Asking permission to do something and apologizing are examples of functions
    c. Identifying a person, place, or thing is considered a notion and not a function
    d. Reporting or denying actions, events, or statements is not a function example

35. According to the Notional-Functional teaching approach, the student needs to express three different types of meanings. Which of the following is NOT one of these?

    a. Modal
    b. Functional
    c. Notional
    d. Conceptual

36. Which is true about general principles for teaching American Sign Language (ASL)?

a. Students should not be required to use ASL until they have learned enough
b. Teachers should use sequential order, but not cumulative or spiral orders
c. Students should be taught expressive skills before learning receptive skills
d. The structures and emphases used for teaching should be conversational

37. Which is true about general principles for teaching American Sign Language (ASL)?

a. Teachers and students should begin using slower rates than normal conversations
b. Teachers should be more active while students should absorb as much as they can
c. Teachers of ASL should check the students' comprehension and mastery regularly
d. Teachers should permit students to use other non-ASL languages in the classroom

38. Which is true about general principles for teaching American Sign Language (ASL)?

a. The teacher should focus on the vocabulary found in school textbooks
b. It is important for ASL teachers to include cultural practices/behaviors
c. Presenting dialogues to the class is not an effective way to teach ASL
d. Initiating conversations has not been found effective for teaching ASL

39. Which is true about general principles for teaching American Sign Language (ASL)?

a. The teaching of ASL should be oriented toward acquisition rather than learning
b. Teachers should prohibit students from generating new combinations of signs
c. Teachers of ASL should limit student creativity to build a strong sign foundation
d. Which activities ASL teachers assign do not matter as long as they are using ASL

40. Among methods used for teaching ASL, which was developed the latest?

a. The Grammar-Translation Method
b. The Notional-Functional Approach
c. The Audio-Lingual/Army Method
d. The Direct Experience Method

41. To address embarrassment and self-consciousness of new ASL students who are reluctant to start signing, which teacher strategy would be most effective?

a. Give the students lists of common vocabulary words to encourage them
b. Disregard minor mistakes; allow gradual development of expressive skills
c. Focus instruction on grammatical forms the students need to learn most
d. Give drills in class, and have students memorize brief dialogues using ASL

42. Which of the following represent(s) disadvantages of using the Vocabulary Method for teaching ASL?

a. Students can too easily get the syntax of sentences in the wrong order
b. Students can get "stuck" with using one sign for multiple word meanings
c. These are both disadvantages of using the Vocabulary Method with ASL
d. Neither of these is a disadvantage of using this method for teaching ASL

43. Among the following language evaluation methods, which would offer the advantage of normative comparisons?

    a.   Self-evaluation
    b.   Peer evaluation
    c.   Teacher-made
    d.   Standardized

44. To design a program combining Special Education and Bilingual Education, which is NOT one of three factors the educator(s) must consider for each individual student?

    a.   The student's level of adaptive behaviors
    b.   The student's intellectual/cognitive ability
    c.   The student's proficiency in both languages
    d.   The student's individual degree of disability

45. What is true of factors influencing program placement decisions for bilingual exceptional students?

    a.   The student's age is less important than the age at the onset of disability
    b.   Language used to test ability and achievement is as important as method
    c.   The student's academic achievement matters more than cognitive ability
    d.   Whether a student has one disability or multiple disabilities is not a factor

46. Which is accurate regarding program placement considerations for deaf students using ASL?

    a.   The student's language skills levels upon beginning school are irrelevant
    b.   Language input the student receives at home is considered immaterial
    c.   The degree of language involvement due to disability must be assessed
    d.   The student's levels of adaptive behaviors should not affect placement

47. Which of the following is NOT a variable to be reflected in program placement decisions for exceptional bilingual students?

    a.   The language that will be used during instruction
    b.   The type and nature of instruction to be offered
    c.   The person who delivers the instruction
    d.   These are all variables placements should reflect

48. What is true about deciding on program placements for bilingual exceptional students?

    a.   It is not necessary to specify how long the instruction will last
    b.   The culture in the student's home environment is significant
    c.   Individual student's learning style does not impact placement
    d.   Placements are decided regardless of the student's social maturity

49. Which statement is correct regarding the instruction of bilingual exceptional students?

    a.   Instruction should always be delivered in the student's more proficient language
    b.   Instruction should be delivered in the student's weaker language to strengthen it
    c.   Instruction should be delivered in both languages in order to achieve equal balance
    d.   Instruction should be delivered regardless of the cultural context or its relevance

50. What is accurate regarding the selection, adaptation, and modification of instructional materials for Deaf ASL-using students and other exceptional bilingual students?

    a. It is best when modifying materials to adapt all of the materials simultaneously

    b. Trial-and-error of materials/adaptations is too "hit-or-miss" and to be avoided

    c. Consistency in evaluating materials and documenting effective ones is needed

    d. The way adaptations of materials are implemented does not affect instruction

51. A teacher wants to assess her high school ASL II students' ability to use descriptive classifiers. Which of the following would be the best way to evaluate this?

    a. Observing video recordings of the students interviewing one another on leisure activities

    b. Assigning dialogues with descriptive classifiers for the students to memorize and present

    c. Giving students a printed test to identify rules for ASL descriptive classifiers, using English

    d. Having students view a video of people's interactions and then describe these using ASL

52. Which statement most accurately represents the status of incorporating Deaf culture into mainstream education relative to the educational inclusion mandates of the IDEA?

    a. Mainstreaming Deaf students inadvertently caused a reciprocal inclusion of Deaf culture

    b. Mainstreaming Deaf students created an absence of and need for including Deaf culture

    c. Mainstreaming Deaf students has polarized Deaf and hearing cultures due to differences

    d. Mainstreaming Deaf students has not had any effect on Deaf culture's inclusion in school

53. Which of the following is true regarding the history and development of ASL?

    a. In 1867, no schools for the Deaf in America were teaching American Sign Language

    b. ASL became the primary way of educating Deaf American students during the 1990s

    c. By 1907 every single school for the Deaf in America was teaching students using ASL

    d. The Congress of Milan in 1880 prompted a change from teaching speech to signing

54. Regarding pluralizing nouns in ASL, what is most accurate about several ways of direct pluralization without using numbers or quantifiers?

    a. Sweeping is an infrequently used method to pluralize personal pronouns

    b. Reduplication in the same place always turns processes into plural nouns

    c. Repositioning a classifier can indicate plural by indicating multiple objects

    d. An inflection to the standard sign movement does not represent a plural

55. In American Sign Language (ASL), a "predicate" *best* relates to which of the following?

    a. A verb

    b. A topic

    c. A time

    d. A comment

56. In American Sign Language (ASL) syntax, if you translated the signs into English, which English translation represents correct signing to say "I am a student"?

    a. "I student"

    b. "Student I"

    c. "I student I"

    d. All of these

57. What one calls "subject-verb agreement" in English grammar is which of the below in ASL?

    a.   Subject-verb agreement is essentially the same
    b.   Subject-verb agreement is actually not an issue
    c.   Subject-verb agreement is indicated differently
    d.   Subject-verb agreement is just "verb agreement"

58. In ASL, you show that a verb is either the subject or object of the sentence by

    a.   changing the place where you make the sign
    b.   changing the direction your palm is pointing
    c.   doing either one or both of these things
    d.   doing neither one of these things

59. What is true about using verb signs in American Sign Language (ASL)?

    a.   Some verb signs can be modified to mean their opposites
    b.   Only a different sign can express the opposite of any verb
    c.   Any verb sign can mean the opposite by adding a negative
    d.   There is a specific "opposite" sign for using with verb signs

60. Among phonological parameters in American Sign Language, which of the following words are differentiated in signing only by a different orientation of the palm?

    a.   "onion" vs. "apple"
    b.   "want" vs. "freeze"
    c.   "mom" vs. "dad"
    d.   "girl" vs. "remember"

61. Among these ASL signs, which pair uses the same movement but a different handshape?

    a.   "sit" vs. "train"
    b.   "fingerspell" vs. "mom"
    c.   "now" vs. "can"
    d.   "remember" vs. "not"

62. In ASL morphology, which type of morpheme changes the meaning related to the part of speech of the word to which it is attached?

    a.   A free morpheme
    b.   A bound morpheme
    c.   An inflectional morpheme
    d.   A derivational morpheme

63. Which is correct according to the Hold-Movement-Hold model or theory in ASL?

    a.   The holds are considered phonemes and the movements are transitions between them
    b.   The movements are considered phonemes and the holds are the punctuations between
    c.   Neither the holds nor movements are considered phonemes; they are both morphemes
    d.   The holds and the movements are both considered to be phonemes in this model/theory

64. Which of the following is the best example of an ASL noun-verb pair that changes the meaning of the noun?

    a. "Sit – chair"

    b. "Teach – teacher"

    c. "Open – book"

    d. "Again – often"

65. Of the following, which is an example of using the Frozen register in speech or sign?

    a. The President making a speech during a press conference

    b. A class reciting the Pledge of Allegiance to the flag of the USA

    c. A car salesman describing models' features to a customer

    d. The conversation in a small group of longtime close friends

66. Which of these communicative registers would be hardest for someone who is not a native ASL user to understand when observing it among others?

    a. Intimate

    b. Casual

    c. Formal

    d. Frozen

67. In terms of ASL syntax, which of the following is LEAST likely to be correctly signed to mean "I washed my car last week"?

    a. "Week-past car wash me"

    b. "Week-past me wash car"

    c. "Me wash car week-past"

    d. All are correct ASL syntax

68. What is most accurate regarding when to use fingerspelling when communicating in ASL?

    a. All of the different kinds of flowers already have ASL signs and need no fingerspelling

    b. Place names of stores, restaurants, cities, and states commonly must be fingerspelled

    c. Persons and also pets have name signs, so it is unnecessary to fingerspell their names

    d. Name brands and titles are fingerspelled, but there are ASL signs for foods and animals

69. Which of the following is true about conversation maintenance techniques when communicating in ASL?

    a. There is a special sign to ask signers to slow down, separate from the general sign for "slow"

    b. Asking a native ASL signer to slow down while signing is considered insulting by Deaf people

    c. If you don't understand a sign, wait for additional signs/information before you sign "HEY"

    d. You should use the sign for "HEY" immediately if you don't recognize a sign someone uses

70. Which of the following would be considered a discourse marker among Deaf ASL users?

    a. Tapping on the table/floor to get somebody's attention

    b. Waving an arm/hand in the air to get people's attention

    c. Types of signaling, communication acts, methods/norms

    d. These are all considered to be discourse markers in ASL

71. Which of the following is true regarding contact signing?

    a. Contact signing is a distinct language, separate from ASL
    b. Contact signing differs from Pidgin Signed English (PSE)
    c. Contact signing is to help deaf and hearing communicate
    d. Contact signing is the language some signers use at home

72. What is correct about psycholinguistic aspects of American Sign Language?

    a. Because ASL is seen and not heard, it is not subject to regional dialects
    b. The educated Deaf use more English forms in ASL than ASL structure
    c. In the Deaf community, SES is not considered an influence on signing
    d. The Deaf community disregards age, race, or gender as affecting ASL

73. In signing, what does the acronym SEE stand for?

    a. Signing Exact English
    b. Seeing Essential English
    c. Both
    d. Neither

74. The SEE methods of signing, such as SEE 1 and SEE 2, are which of the below?

    a. Invented sign systems
    b. Natural sign systems
    c. The same as ASL
    d. None of these

75. In the SEE 2 signing method, what are the signs mainly based upon?

    a. The "2 of 3" rule
    b. English syllables
    c. Both of these
    d. Neither of these

76. Which of the following best characterizes Deaf culture relative to hearing culture?

    a. Deaf culture is essentially the same as hearing culture with a few minor differences
    b. Deaf culture is a distinct culture incorporated in and influenced by the larger culture
    c. Deaf culture is completely separate from and is not affected by the hearing culture
    d. Deaf culture is a larger influence upon the hearing culture rather than the opposite

77. Which of the following statements is correct regarding signing and interpreting?

    a. Signing and interpreting are interchangeable synonyms
    b. Anyone who can sign can also interpret sign languages
    c. Someone who can interpret signing can also use signing
    d. These mean different things but can never be separate

78. What is true about Deaf college student preferences in communicating with English-speaking hearing persons?

    a. Most Deaf college students prefer using live interpreters over real-time captioning typists
    b. Real-time caption stenographers are generally not as accurate as sign language interpreters
    c. Deaf college students who use sign language are unlikely to have good command of English
    d. There are many Deaf, signing college students who prefer real-time caption stenographers

79. **When attending to a Deaf person who is signing, you should *focus* most on the signer's**
    a. face
    b. hands
    c. chest area
    d. All these at once

80. **If two signers having a conversation are in your path, which should you do?**
    a. Wait until they finish or pause before walking in between them
    b. Walk between them in a crouch so as not to block their signing
    c. Find a way to walk around them, or go in a different direction
    d. Do not be afraid to walk between them, but at normal speed

81. **Which of the following is true regarding deafness in families?**
    a. Ninety percent of Deaf and hard-of-hearing children have Deaf parents
    b. Ninety percent of Deaf and hard-of-hearing children have hearing parents
    c. Fifty percent of DHH children have hearing parents and 50 percent Deaf parents
    d. Percentages of Deaf/hearing parents cannot be measured accurately

82. **TDD and TTY represent devices that help Deaf people to use which of the below?**
    a. Radios
    b. Televisions
    c. Telephones
    d. Computers

83. **Which is true about TDD and TTY?**
    a. These terms differ in age and technology, but not in purpose
    b. These terms differ in that only one of them is used by the Deaf
    c. These terms are for different devices used for different reasons
    d. These terms are unlikely to be used interchangeably by the Deaf

84. **If you are a hearing person communicating with a Deaf person using a live ASL interpreter, at whom should you look during the conversation?**
    a. You should always look only at the Deaf person
    b. You should always look only at the ASL interpreter
    c. You should divide your gaze equally between the two
    d. You should mainly look at the Deaf person, but not 100 percent

85. **Relative to Deaf culture, which is most true of an adult who has just lost his or her hearing?**
    a. This person automatically becomes a member of the Deaf community via hearing loss
    b. This person is still a member of the Hearing World who has just become unable to hear
    c. This person is a member of a separate transitional community between hearing and Deaf
    d. This person will develop full Deaf identity and Deaf community membership by learning ASL

86. Historically, Deaf people have encountered discrimination relative to being hired. What else is true about the history of workplace discrimination against the Deaf?

    a.   Deaf people have been offered equal opportunities for job-related training
    b.   When hired, Deaf people have had equal access to information on the job
    c.   Deaf people have received fewer opportunities to advance their careers
    d.   Deaf people have been promoted equally to management/supervision

87. What is the most correct statement about the culturally Deaf in America?

    a.   Culturally Deaf Americans consider themselves to have a disability
    b.   If they could become hearing, most culturally Deaf would refuse it
    c.   Deafness is a problem to be solved to the culturally Deaf in the USA
    d.   The culturally Deaf accept their deafness but do not think it is good

88. Which is true about the clinical/pathological or medical model of deafness?

    a.   People who subscribe to this view feel that deafness involves culture and language
    b.   People who subscribe to this view see deafness as a difference, but not a disability
    c.   People who subscribe to this view and are also Deaf are likely to be "culturally Deaf"
    d.   People who subscribe to this view and are also Deaf are likely not to be fluent in ASL

89. Which is the most accurate statement about culturally Deaf people in the USA?

    a.   They give much more biographical and social information upon introductions
    b.   They are less likely to greet one another by hugging than hearing people are
    c.   They tend to take less time saying good-bye to each other than the hearing
    d.   They usually prefer to socialize in the living room rather than in the kitchen

90. Which of the following is true about audism?

    a.   Audism is a technique for enhancing residual hearing in the HOH
    b.   Audism is a specific method for educating the Deaf and the HOH
    c.   Audism is based on assuming that speech and hearing are better
    d.   Audism is a belief system that tends to support Deaf culture/ASL

91. Of the following, which is NOT identified as a level or type of existing audism?

    a.   Informational
    b.   Institutional
    c.   Ideological
    d.   Individual

92. Which of the following is the most accurate definition of linguicism?

    a.   Emphasis on the importance of language whether spoken or signed
    b.   A lack of equality between/among groups using different languages
    c.   The practice of defining various social groups according to languages
    d.   A philosophy of studying languages as a means for studying cultures

93. What statement is generally most true of terminology preferences relative to deafness?

    a.   The hearing population tends to use "Deaf" more than "hearing-impaired"
    b.   Deaf people generally are not offended at being called "hearing-impaired"
    c.   People with hearing tend to think it's rude to describe somebody as "Deaf"
    d.   Hearing people often find the term "hearing-impaired" politically incorrect

94. **When a hearing person meets a deaf person, which of these is correct?**
    a. The hearing person should give as much background information as the deaf do
    b. The hearing person should give more background information than the deaf do
    c. The hearing person should identify the school s/he attended as it is Deaf custom
    d. The hearing person should identify any deaf relatives as motivation to learn ASL

95. **The Deaf President Now (DPN) event in Washington, D.C. in 1988 was**
    a. a movement to allow a Deaf candidate to become President of the USA
    b. a movement to find a Deaf candidate for President of Gallaudet University
    c. a protest against the policies for electing University presidents in the USA
    d. a protest against selection from three finalists of the one hearing candidate

96. **Which organization first served to unite various groups concerned with DHH issues?**
    a. National Association of the Deaf (NAD)
    b. American Society for Deaf Children (ASDC)
    c. The Consumer Action Network (CAN)
    d. American Sign Language Teachers Association (ASLTA)

97. **"A huge giant is stalking through a small village of wee people, who are scattering through the streets, trying to escape the ugly creature. The giant notices one particularly beautiful blonde woman scampering down the cobble-stoned street. He stretches out his clumsy arm and sweeps her up, then stares in wonder at the slight, shivering figure in his palm. "You are so beautiful," he exclaims. The young woman looks up in fear. "I would never hurt you," he signs, "I love you! We should get MARRIED." Producing the sign MARRY, he crushes her. The giant then laments, "See, oralism is better." (*The Signs of Language,* Klima and Bellugi 1988, excerpted in Vicars, 2006) What is NOT a reason this joke works when told in ASL?**
    a. It is active visually
    b. It champions oralism
    c. It is funny linguistically
    d. It uses irony for humor

98. **Which of the following laws dictates that private employers and state and local government employers may not practice employment discrimination against the deaf?**
    a. Title I of the Americans with Disabilities Act (ADA)
    b. Title II of the Americans with Disabilities Act (ADA)
    c. Title V, Section 504 of the Rehabilitation Act of 1973
    d. Title V, Section 501 of the Rehabilitation Act of 1973

Answer Key and Explanations

1. C: BICS are the skills used in informal social conversation. They are not cognitively demanding, involving such simple cognitions as naming things, expressing negatives, et cetera. They do not include new ideas and words, but rely on known concepts, vocabulary, and syntax. They do not apply to novel situations, but to daily routines, such as dressing, eating, playing, bathing, et cetera.

2. C: Cummins proposed that experience with learning one's first language, and/or with learning a second language, promotes underlying proficiency in both languages. Therefore experience with a second language does promote first-language proficiency, and experience with the first language does promote second-language proficiency. It is not true that only experience with the first language promotes second-language proficiency.

3. B: The SUP, or Separate Underlying Proficiency, approach posits that people learn their first language in a separate, unrelated process from learning a second language. This theory does not hold that learning one's first language facilitates learning a second one, or that learning a second language improves the first one. It finds that there is no synergy or relation between the acquisition of first and second languages.

4. B: Language is learned best when the affective filter is low. The affective filter is a "screen of emotion" most related to embarrassment or self-consciousness, which can prevent the learner from communicative risk-taking and thus inhibit language acquisition. Having a high affective filter would interfere with learning. The affective filter does not distort word meanings; it influences one's attitudes toward learning language. It does not promote using language socially, but can impede this if it is excessive.

5. A: The initial "P" in PEPSI stands for the "Pre-Production Stage" of language development, also called the "Silent Period" wherein there is no language production and minimal receptive language comprehension. This stage does not include productive or proficient use of language. It is a stage that exists prior to fluent language use, but the "P" does not stand for "Prior to Fluency."

6. A: The Early Production stage in the PEPSI model of language development is characterized expressively by the production of one- or two-word phrases. Simple sentences are not produced until the next stage; complex sentences are not used until two stages later. Excellent comprehension characterizes only a fully fluent stage of language development.

7. D: In the PEPSI model, the "S" stands for "Speech" in the Speech Emergence Stage, wherein simple sentences are produced, and comprehension is better than in the previous stage. "Silent" is part of PEPSI's first, Pre-Production stage, also called the Silent Period. "Short" is not a term used in PEPSI's stage names. However, the one- and two-word utterances produced in the second stage are shorter than the simple sentences produced in the third stage. "Simple" relates to the simple sentences produced in the Speech Emergence Stage, but the "S" represents "Speech" rather than "Simple."

8. D: In this model, the "I" in PEPSI represents "Intermediate" in the Intermediate Fluency Stage, wherein comprehension improves, and both sentences produced and errors made are more complex than before. This model and this initial in the acronym do not refer to anything individualized, to the learner's intelligence, or to the learner's independence of language production.

9. A: The concept of "input + 1" (Krashen) refers to the optimum linguistic input for language acquisition, which is just slightly higher in level than the learner's present language level. It does not refer to input plus one more speakers, to speech plus one more medium, or to input plus one additional language variable. It relates to Vygotsky's Zone of Proximal Development, wherein optimal learning occurs with exposure to someone at a level just slightly higher than that of the learner.

10. C: Noam Chomsky has theorized in his cognitive-Gestalt orientation that we are born with a Language Acquisition Device (LAD) enabling us to learn grammar unconsciously and generate rules from it. Krashen and Terrell are known for Language Acquisition Theory, positing that acquisition and learning are separate processes, that learning develops a monitor, and that language development progresses in a natural order. Both also subscribe to the Natural communicative approach. Galyean supports a Humanistic communicative approach treating the whole person, beginning with the individual, and extending to the group, and including physical activity, art, and music.

11. B: Even tiny babies 3 months or younger will respond to familiar and unfamiliar voices in these ways. Newborns are aware of sounds and attend to them, waking, startling or crying at noises, quieting at new sounds, and listening to nearby speech. They do not start turning and smiling immediately at birth, but at some time between birth and three months. Developments beyond these are normal at 4-6 and 7-12 months.

12. C: Toddlers 1-2 years old can normally follow two-step instructions, for example, "Pick up the truck and put it in the toy box." Children aged 7-12 months should be able to follow one-step instructions, for example, "Push the truck," and answer simple questions, for example, "Where's the truck?". And 3-4-year-olds can understand simple questions with "Who...?", "What...?", and "Where...?". By 5-6 years old, children can normally answer simple questions about stories they hear.

13. A: It is normal for babies to smile, coo, and differentiate their cries at 3 months old. The baby is not developmentally delayed as babies normally start to babble between 4 and 6 months old. The absence of vocal play at three months does not indicate hearing loss or other developmental disability. The baby is not developmentally advanced as s/he is not doing anything unusual for the age of three months, such as uttering first words or babbling.

14. B: Children between 1 and 2 years old typically develop the expressive ability to make two-word questions and statements. Children 7-12 months old begin speaking their first words, such as "mama," "da-da," "night-night," "bye-bye," "doggie," and "baby", but usually do not utter two-word constructions yet. Children between 2 and 3 years old commonly can make three-word utterances and develop noticeably larger vocabularies. Children between 3 and 4 years old typically can speak fluently and clearly in sentences of four or more words.

15. D: Physician Geronimo Cardano of Padua, Italy, proposed in the 16th century that deaf people could learn language by using signs. In the 17th century (1620), Juan Pablo de Bonet, a Spanish priest and deaf education pioneer, published the first book on teaching deaf people sign language, including a manual alphabet. (It should also be noted that deaf people had previously developed signing systems naturally.) Pedro Ponce de Leon, a Spanish Benedictine monk, formulated signs based on the Spanish alphabet in the 16th century. Ancient Greek philosopher Aristotle believed that people could not learn without hearing.

16. A: The Abbé Charles Michel de L'Epée founded the first free school for the deaf in Paris in 1755. He developed a sign system based on signs already used by deaf Parisians, and also created signs for spoken French. Samuel Heinicke founded the first governmentally recognized public school for the deaf in Leipzig in 1778. He did not use signs, but speechreading. Thomas Hopkins Gallaudet founded the first school for the deaf in America in Hartford, Connecticut in 1817. Gallaudet invited sign language teacher Laurent Clerc from France to become the first deaf sign language teacher in the United States.

17. D: All of these developments were directly influenced by deaf athletes. The first deaf baseball player in the Major League, William "Dummy" Hoy, caused umpires to adopt hand signals for "strike," "safe," and "out." Gallaudet University's football team produced the innovation of the huddle to keep opposing teams from eavesdropping on the quarterback. At the first World Games for the Deaf, held in Paris, France in 1924, the international athletes developed Gestuno for use at the sports event, which has now been renamed International Sign and is still used today.

18. A: Research finds that babies can learn to communicate physically using sign language as early as 6-8 months, much earlier than they can communicate using speech. Research also finds that the language development of babies and young children who learn sign language is stronger than that of those who do not.

19. C: Researchers have discovered that even when they see imperfect ASL use, which is common, children still produce ASL with perfect grammar. The researchers find this is evidence that children's brains contain inherent abilities for generating grammar. Other researchers have found that when children are exposed to manually encoded English, but not to ASL, they are likely to generate structures spontaneously that are very similar to ASL.

20. D: Researchers such as Emmorey (1993) have found that people who were fluent in ASL performed better on visual and visual-spatial imagery tasks. They also concluded that this enhanced imaging ability was not limited to deaf ASL signers and was not due to hearing loss, because hearing people who had deaf parents and were fluent in ASL also performed better on these tasks. The researchers observed a relationship between the requirements of ASL and enhanced visual-spatial imagery abilities.

21. B: American Sign Language has significant differences not only from British and French Sign Languages, but from others as well. Sign languages, like spoken languages, vary among different geographical regions and countries. ASL shares considerably more vocabulary with FSL because of the influence of French sign-language teacher Laurent Clerc, who taught FSL to American students at the first American school for the deaf founded by Thomas Gallaudet when Gallaudet brought him to America in 1817. ASL was also influenced by early deaf Americans' natural signing. ASL, BSL, and FSL are not mutually comprehensible.

22. C: Immersion methods/programs for learning second languages are similar to two-way methods/programs in that both are bilingual education programs wherein all students receive instruction in both primary and secondary languages. Submersion methods are "sink-or-swim" approaches which place students speaking minority languages into classes with native speakers of the majority language, and they are expected to learn as much as possible. In one-way methods, students speaking minority languages are taught the majority language, but majority-language students are not taught the minority language, so these are not bilingual. Direct methods like Berlitz are non-communicative and exclusively use the second language being learned.

23. D: This is an example of both interference, when one's native language (especially in vocabulary) interferes with the use of a second language; and of an interlanguage, a transition stage wherein a second-language learner develops a personal language which is somewhere between the native and second languages, but is not either one. In English, "deranged" commonly denotes insanity, but the French cognate "déranger" commonly means to inconvenience someone. Fossilization is a process wherein a second-language learner gets "stuck" repeating certain errors in the second language despite many years of instruction, advanced proficiency, and few other errors.

24. B: The ideas and interactions a particular community finds most significant are likely to be reflected in that community's language. Social traditions are typically passed on to succeeding generations through behavior and oral more than written language. Speaking the same language does not dictate that residents of a community also hold the same moral beliefs. Linguistic structures inevitably evolve over time due to multiple influences and thus are not preserved unchanged by a community's cultural traditions.

25. D: The typical way deaf culture is passed from one generation to the next is through the in-person/face-to-face communication among community members. Family communications are vitally important, but the whole Deaf culture would not be as effectively transmitted only within families as throughout communities. Deaf communication is as interactional as hearing communication, the only general difference being that it does not use hearing; thus deaf people transmit culture by communicating rather than using pictures. Culture is transmitted more through interpersonal communication than written records, by both hearing and deaf people.

26. B: Learning strategies taught in the CALLA are not categorized as academic, because these strategies are taught within the academic subject areas themselves. Cognitive strategies include such things as note-taking, inferring, summarizing, and self-reflecting. Metacognitive strategies involve executive functions such as classifying, planning, and self-monitoring. Social-affective strategies include such processes as asking questions, peer tutoring, and cooperative learning activities.

27. C: The Home Language Survey is a form given to a student's parents, which they fill out to provide information to the school about their child's language background. It is not typically completed by a school social worker or a language arts teacher. (Parents speaking a foreign/minority language might receive assistance from someone who can translate their responses into English on the form, or they might complete it in their language, to be translated into English.) This form is not optional for all students: It is required for every student identified as having Limited English Proficiency (LEP).

28. A: Psychologist Lev Vygotsky subscribed to social constructivism, the theory that we actively create our own learning, knowledge, and worldviews. He formulated his social-interactionist theory that learners construct new learning, including language, through socially mediated interactions. Today's social interaction perspectives on language learning are based on Vygotsky's theory. Noam Chomsky's theory of language acquisition is a Nativist theory; Chomsky believes people are born with an internal Language Acquisition Device (LAD) enabling them to generate grammatical rules. Stephen Krashen who proposed the input hypothesis and Tracy Terrell with their Natural Approach are both considered Nativists, assuming natural intrinsic mechanisms for language acquisition. (Krashen, like Vygotsky, emphasizes the importance of interaction in second language acquisition. However, Krashen's belief in innate mechanisms classifies him as Nativist.)

29. C: Both hearing people and deaf people wish to instill the same values in their children. Deaf culture finds ASL mastery important, but most hearing cultures generally do not. Excellent storytelling skills are prized more in Deaf culture, as they are a primary way to transmit the culture. Most literate hearing cultures rely more on written records, while developing societies with little or no writing systems use oral history. Thinking and speaking like hearing people is taken for granted in hearing cultures; in Deaf culture, it is viewed negatively.

30. B: Socialization is a process necessary to a child's growth and development. Socialization is much easier when students share a common language. Residential schools for the deaf in America most often emphasize ASL. Some emphasize Total Communication, speechreading, or other methods, but at each school all the students are likely to use the same language, facilitating socialization. Residential schools are of crucial importance to transmitting Deaf culture and language. They provide Deaf students with Deaf role models, which they are much less likely to find in mainstream education. These schools also offer more opportunities to participate in sports activities, social and academic clubs, et cetera on an equal basis with their peers.

31. C: The Direct Method was formulated by Charles Berlitz for teaching foreign languages and adapted by Rochester Institute of Technology, N.Y.'s National Technical Institute for the Deaf (NTID) as the Direct Experience Method. These methods teach both receptive and expressive language skills; uses objects, pictures, and demonstrations to teach concrete vocabulary; and teaches abstract vocabulary by associating concepts. Direct methods do not use equal amounts of the native and target second language; they use the target language exclusively. They stress the importance of grammar and pronunciation. DEM is designed around question-and-answer student-teacher interactions, not rote repetition.

32. B: The Natural Approach stresses the importance of using everyday communicative situations in learning a second language, including ASL, since these are the situations in which they will use the language the most. Based on theories of second language acquisition, Krashen stated that students should be as relaxed as possible for optimal learning. He placed emphasis on acquisition of the language as opposed to analysis of it. He also emphasized that students did not need to say anything in the second language until they felt ready to use it.

33. A: In the Notional-Functional approach, general notions are abstract concepts such as time, space, quantity, quality, existence, et cetera, and are used to express thoughts, ideas, and feelings. Specific notions are equivalent to contexts or situations, like education, health, travel, shopping, leisure activities; and personal identifiers, such as names, addresses, and phone numbers.

34. B: Asking permission to do something and apologizing for something are two examples of functions in the Notional-Functional teaching approach. The authors of this approach, Van Ek and Alexander, have identified approximately 70 distinct functions of language, not seven. Identification of something is also a function, not a notion. Reporting or denying actions, events, or statements are also examples of functions, as are accepting or declining invitations to do something and complaining about something.

35. C: Notional is not one of the three types of meaning the student needs to express according to the Notional-Functional approach. Notions are defined as general, abstract concepts or specific contexts or situations. A syllabus may be designated "notional." The three types of meaning to be expressed in this approach are Modal, the degree of likelihood (examples of modal linking verbs are *can*, *may*, and *should*); Functional, such as an utterance's social purpose; and Conceptual, how forms within a sentence express relationships of meanings, or communicative function categories.

36. D: When teaching ASL to students, teachers should use the same structures and emphases in the ASL they use as are normally used during ASL conversations. Students should be encouraged to begin using ASL right away to learn by doing and for practice. Teachers should use all three orders (sequential, cumulative, and spiral) in teaching ASL. (Sequential is linear, cumulative builds new learning upon prior learning, and spiral is recursive, beginning with simple concepts and periodically revisiting to expand on them.) Students should always learn receptive skills first before expressive skills. This is the way hearing children learn language. Without reception there is no comprehension, limiting expression.

37. C: Teachers of ASL should be sure they regularly monitor how well their students understand the new language and the degree of mastery of it they are achieving. Teachers and students should not begin by using slower rates than normal conversations in ASL. Teachers should present material at normal rates, and students should be instructed to use signs at normal speeds and/or aim to attain these. Teachers should not be more active than students, nor should students be more passive in absorbing information. Rather, teachers should invite and require students' active participation for optimal learning. ASL teachers should also instruct students to leave other, non-ASL languages outside of the ASL classroom.

38. B: It is important for ASL teachers to incorporate cultural practices and behaviors in their lessons because ASL is a primary way in which Deaf culture is transmitted. Teachers should focus not on vocabulary found in academic texts used in schools, but rather on vocabulary used in everyday situations, to facilitate students' learning to communicate in ASL. Presenting dialogues to the class, and initiating conversations wherein the students use ASL, are both effective practices for teaching ASL according to experts.

39. A: It is true among general principles for teaching ASL that instruction should be oriented to acquisition rather than learning. In this case, learning refers to the formal academic knowledge of a language, and acquisition to the natural, unconscious process of acquiring language through using it in actual conversation. Teachers should never prohibit students, even beginners, from forming new combinations of signs they have learned; they should encourage this as it facilitates both acquisition and fluency. Similarly, they should never limit student creativity in signing but should promote it. Which activities the teacher assigns do matter; they should be meaningful to the students for them to be engaged in acquiring and using the language most naturally.

40. D: The Direct Experience Method was the 1980s adaptation by the National Technical Institute for the Deaf (NTID) at Rochester Institute of Technology (RIT), N.Y. of Berlitz' (1878) Direct Method for teaching foreign languages. The Grammar-Translation Method, a traditional approach, was originally used in the 19th century to teach "dead" languages like Latin, so listening comprehension and spoken communication were not emphasized. The Audio-Lingual or Army Method began after World War II, consisting of intensive language courses using listening to dialogue sentences, memorizing phrases, and repeated drills. Used for many aurally-based foreign languages, it was applied to ASL as well. The Notional-Functional Approach, developed by Van Ek and Alexander in 1975, was adopted by the Council of Europe.

41. B: When students display what Krashen (1982) called an "affective filter," an emotional component that can interfere with acquiring a language when it inhibits risking mistakes and/or humiliation, the most effective of the strategies listed would be to allow the student's time to develop their expressive ASL skills gradually, while not excessively correcting insignificant errors in grammar. This is the same approach advocated with young children developing their first/native languages. Academic practices like giving vocabulary lists, teaching grammatical forms, conducting drills, and/or assigning memorization of brief dialogues can be combined with (C), but used alone are less effective because they do not involve actually communicating in ASL and using it in conversations, which best promote ASL acquisition.

42. C: These are both disadvantages of using the Vocabulary Method to teach ASL. By relying overly on vocabulary and word meanings, students can miss the structural differences in ASL and create an ASL sentence with the subject, verb, and object in the wrong order. For example, an English-speaking, new ASL student might sign "car-hit-tree" (subject-verb-object), corresponding to English sentence syntax; but in ASL syntax it should be "tree, car CL: 3-crash-into" (object-subject [CL: 3 is a Classifier handshape including vehicles]-verb-preposition, or Topic-Comment as it is termed in ASL syntax). ASL is a unique language, not a signed transcription of English. Another disadvantage is that students may learn one sign for a word having multiple meanings. Even though the same English word is used for each meaning, in ASL it is crucial to teach different signs for different meanings.

43. D: Standardized tests develop national standards according to the average scores of a sample group of students. Individual students' scores can then be compared to these norms to see how they performed relative to the average normal performance. Self-evaluation promotes objectivity, reflectiveness, and analytical skills in the student, but no normative comparisons. Peer evaluations benefit students with their classmates' feedback and develop objectivity and analysis in the evaluators, but have no norms. Teacher-made evaluations can be individualized for particular students and lessons but are not normative.

44. A: The level(s) of an individual student's adaptive behaviors is one of many factors that should influence decisions in identifying placement for the student. For program design combining Special and Bilingual Education, three main factors to consider for each student are the student's intellectual or cognitive ability levels, the bilingual student's level of proficiency in each language, and the individual student's degree of disability.

45. B: Placement decisions for bilingual exceptional students should be influenced equally by the language and the methodology used to assess the student's intellectual ability and academic achievement, as both affect the results. The student's current age is an equally important influence on placement decisions as the age of onset of the student's disability. The student's cognitive abilities and academic performance are also equally important influences. Additionally, educators should consider whether a student has one disability or multiple disabilities in deciding on program placement. (Note: Deaf students using ASL are automatically both exceptional and bilingual students.)

46. C: When deciding on program placement for exceptional, including deaf, students who are bilingual, including ASL, educators should consider how much the student's disability causes language involvement. They should also consider the levels of the student's language skills upon entry to school, which are relevant influences on placement. The type and amount of linguistic input the student receives at home is another important factor in placement decisions. The student's adaptive behavior levels will also affect placement decisions, as the program should not require many basic skills that an individual student lacks.

47. D: Decisions regarding program placement for exceptional bilingual students should reflect what language will be used to instruct each student, the type of instruction to be given and the nature of the instruction, and who the specific teacher/educator will be to deliver this instruction.

48. B: When deciding on placing a bilingual exceptional student (which de facto includes deaf students using ASL) in an educational program, one factor to consider is the duration of the instruction to be provided. This should be specified as it will affect the placement and the delivery of instruction. Decision-makers should be informed about the culture in the student's home, which will affect the student's educational needs, abilities, interests, and preferences as well as the parents' wishes, which should also be considered. The student's learning style should be assessed to find its best match in instructional methods. Another important factor to influence program placement is the individual student's level of social maturity. Placement fitting this level can largely determine student success in a program.

49. A: When instructing bilingual exceptional students, which includes ASL-using Deaf students, the instruction should always be given in the stronger of the student's two languages. For Deaf students raised using ASL to communicate, ASL is typically the stronger language. Instruction in the student's weaker language is not advisable because language is the primary medium for conveying teaching, including directions the student must understand to follow them and information the student must understand to learn it. Delivering instruction in both languages is more likely to achieve confusion than balance. Teachers must also deliver instruction in a cultural context relevant to the student for the student to understand the teacher's expectations.

50. C: Educators should adopt some constant format or set of rules for evaluating materials so that their judgments are consistent across materials. It is also vital that they document which adaptations, modifications, and/or materials were effective with students so they can use them again with other students having similar needs. When making modifications, teachers should only modify those materials specifically needing them. Experts warn against modifying too many things at once, which can become unmanageable for both teachers and students. Trial-and-error is not to be avoided and is the right choice. Teachers must experiment with various adaptations/materials until they find what works best for each student's education. Instruction *is* affected by the way adaptations of materials are implemented. Implementation should be strategic to provide for the smoothest transitions from old to new materials.

51. D: Classifiers in ASL are signs that indicate general classes or categories of things. Descriptive classifiers are one type of classifiers that specify sizes and shapes of objects and people. The teacher can best assess how well students use these by having them describe interactions they just viewed on video using ASL. Observing recordings of the students interviewing each other about leisure activities is not as effective an assessment because such records may or may not include much use of descriptive classifiers specifically. Assigning memorization and presentation of dialogues does not assess how the students spontaneously, conversationally, and independently use descriptive classifiers. Giving them a test they have to complete using English does not test how they use ASL.

52. A: As Rosen (2006, Columbia University, N.Y.) has pointed out, the intent of the IDEA was to include students with disabilities in regular education; however, its implementation unexpectedly also caused non-Deaf students and general education teachers to become interested in Deaf culture through exposure to mainstreamed Deaf students, and to want to learn ASL to communicate with them, so inclusion became reciprocal. Therefore inclusion did not create a vacuum with no knowledge of Deaf culture, but instead stimulated attainment of that knowledge. Mainstreaming thus has not further polarized the Deaf and hearing's differences, but encouraged communication. As such it has had a decided effect on the inclusion of Deaf culture in public schools.

53. B: It was in the 1990s that ASL again became the dominant way to teach Deaf students in America. In 1867, every single school for the Deaf in America was actually teaching ASL. However, the Congress of Milan in 1880 issued a decision that speech instead of signing should be taught in Deaf schools. Consequently, by 1907, not one single American Deaf school was teaching ASL anymore. Meanwhile, the Total Communication approach developed. Many students abandoned learning in reaction to the difficulty of this method. The Commission on Education of the Deaf addressed the President and Congress in 1988 on the unsatisfactory status of American Deaf

Education. Thereafter, signing returned, becoming the primary mode of teaching Deaf Americans by the 1990s.

54. C: One way to indicate pluralization is to reposition a classifier, for example the CL: 3 for vehicles to mean multiple cars, such that the repositioning shows the equivalent of "a car here, one here, and one here." Sweeping (the hand or fingers) directionally is a common method of pluralizing personal pronouns, such as from "she" to "they" or "it" to "those." Reduplication of a sign in the same location often, but NOT always, changes processes into plural nouns. For example, the process (in English, verb) "teach" becomes the plural noun "teachings" through reduplication, as the process "cancel" becomes "cancellations"; however, the sign for "adopt" is not reduplicated in ASL to mean "adoptions." An inflection, i.e. a change, to the standard sign's movement can indeed represent a plural, e.g. inflecting the sign for "person" makes it "people."

55. D: While "predicate" is associated with "verb" in English, in ASL it has a different meaning. ASL tends to follow a "Time-Topic-Comment" format. The time, which relates to verb tense in English, is established before the sentence is uttered in ASL. The topic in ASL is the counterpart of the sentence subject in English, and the ASL predicate is the comment about the topic.

56. D: These English translations all represent correct ways to sign "I am a student" in ASL. (Pointing or touching an index finger to the chest signs "I.") Note that each version differs from English in that ASL does not use "to be"/verbs indicating states of being or articles, and that there is more flexibility of choice in sign orders using the same signs. In English, using the same words, there are only two acceptable word orders: "I am a student" or "A student am I," less often used and likely to sound strange, if not literary or dramatic. Any other English syntax would require different words.

57. B: There is actually no such thing in ASL as "subject-verb agreement" because verbs are not normally changed to show agreement between subject and verb. It is not the and therefore is not indicated at all. It is not the same as "verb agreement," which does exist in ASL, but ASL "verb agreement" refers to inflecting (changing) a verb to show that it is the subject, or the object, of the sentence. In ASL some verbs, called "agreement verbs," can be inflected to show this, while others cannot. For example, "hate" is an agreement verb while "love" and "like" are "plain [non-agreement] verbs."

58. C: In ASL, you inflect a sign for a verb to show it is the subject, or the object, of the sentence by making the sign in a different location than you usually do; or by changing the orientation of your palm, such as the direction in which it is pointing; or by making both of these changes in the sign at the same time.

59. A: It is true that some ASL verb signs can be modified, or inflected, to mean their opposites. For example, the verb "like," if signed with its orientation reversed, means "don't like." It is hence not true that the opposite of any verb can only be expressed with a separate sign. It is not true that any ASL verb can be reversed in meaning by "adding a negative." There is no specific sign for using with any ASL verb to indicate it's opposite.

60. B: In ASL, the difference between the signs for "want" and "freeze" are shown by using a different palm orientation with a sign that is otherwise the same. The words "onion" vs. "apple" are differentiated by signs with the same handshape but made in different locations. The signs for "mom" vs. "dad," and also for "girl" vs. "remember" use the same handshape but in different locations.

61. C: In ASL, the signs meaning "now" and "can" use the same hand movement, but each has a different handshape. The signs for "sit" and "train" use different hand movements. "Fingerspell" is signed with the same handshape as both "mom" and "dad," but in a different location and with a different palm orientation. The sign for "remember" uses the same handshape as, but in a different location than, the signs for "not" and also for "girl."

62. D: A derivational morpheme in ASL changes the meaning of the part of speech played by the word to which the morpheme attaches. For example, if the derivational morpheme of an added hand movement indicating "chair" is attached to the sign for "sit," the verb becomes transitive (acting on an object) and the meaning changes from just "sit" to "sit [on a] chair." A free morpheme is a meaningful unit by itself which needs no attachments to mean something and cannot be broken down to smaller meaningful parts. A bound morpheme needs to attach to something to acquire meaning, e.g. the plural "s" ending attached to the sign "cat." An inflectional morpheme never makes a new word, but a different form of the same word, such as when "teach" becomes "teacher."

63. D: According to the Hold-Movement-Hold Model or Theory, the most common form of expression in ASL is a sequence of a hold followed by a movement followed by another hold. Both the holds and the movements are considered to be phonemes (not morphemes) according to this model or theory. A few examples of signs using the HMH format include: "parents," "prince," "king," "queen," "lord," "Jesus," "discuss," "body," "regular," and "home."

64. C: The pairing of "open" and "book" is an example in ASL where adding the verb "open" changes the meaning of the noun "book." Adding the hand movement for the object noun "chair" changes the meaning of the verb "sit." (These are typically called "noun-verb pairs" in ASL, even though in this example the verb "open" comes first; it is a modifier changing the noun's meaning.) Adding either the ending meaning person, or the affix indicating agency, to the verb "teach" changes its meaning to that of the noun "teacher." "Again" is an adverb whose meaning is changed to that of the adverb "often" by adding a hand movement, signifying a concept like "again and again" or "again many times."

65. B: Reciting the Pledge of Allegiance, singing the National Anthem, reciting the 12 Steps of Alcoholics Anonymous at a meeting, a Catholic priest and congregation reciting the Mass, et cetera are examples of frozen register in that the words or signs used are constant, unchanging across instances. The President making a speech during a press conference is an example of formal register. A car salesman describing the features of various models to a customer is an example of the consultative register. The conversation among longtime close friends in a small group is an example of the casual register.

66. A: The intimate register is used among people who are most familiar with one another. It uses the most "code," such as nicknames for people and expressions for actions/behaviors, the most contractions, and the least repetition, explanation, clarification, and planned organization. The casual register shares these characteristics, assuming much shared knowledge among participants. The intimate register assumes even more privately/idiosyncratically shared knowledge, such that outsiders would not understand many terms. The formal register typically is used when addressing large groups of people, by those in official offices, and with less familiar others. Communication is slower, more carefully articulated, more organized, and more one-way than two-way. The frozen register involves a script, as in religious services or when saying the Pledge of Allegiance to the American flag.

67. C: It would not be correct ASL syntax to begin the sentence with "me." ASL does not begin sentences with what is identified as the grammatical subject in English, and does not use English's

"Subject-Verb" syntax. ASL uses "Topic-Comment" syntax. Moreover, ASL uses "Time-Topic-Comment" order; for example when signing about the past or the future, the time is established at the beginning of the sentence, *before* stating the topic and the comment about the topic. Thus the signer could make either "me" or "car" the topic, and "wash car" or "wash me" the comment; but in either case, signing "week-past" would always come first.

68. B: It is true that when communicating in ASL, people commonly have to use fingerspelling (manual alphabets) to indicate place names, such as of stores or restaurants, and even cities and states do not have signs and must be spelled. It is not true that all flowers have ASL signs already; there is only an ASL sign for "rose," but none for any other flower types. While some persons and pets (particularly Deaf, ASL-using persons and their pets) have name signs, not all do, and with those who do, you are not likely to know it immediately and would fingerspell it. While name brands and titles are fingerspelled, so are many foods and animals, of which there are thousands with no corresponding ASL signs.

69. D: If you do not recognize or understand a sign used by a Deaf person, you should immediately stop him/her by using the "HEY" sign to alert them to your need for clarification. You should NOT wait for additional signs or other information, because if you let the signer continue when you have already missed something, you will likely become lost as to what follows, and the signer is just wasting time and energy rather than communicating. If you are just learning ASL and a Deaf person signs too fast for you to follow, you should ask the person to slow down. This does not involve a special or separate sign; it is the same sign that generally means "slow" in ASL. Degrees of slowness can be indicated by the distance and speed of the hand/arm movements. Asking someone to slow down is not considered insulting by Deaf people, especially when asked by those not fluent in ASL, as it facilitates communication.

70. D: A discourse marker is a term for things ASL users commonly do to get others' attention in discourse/conversations. Synonyms include types of signaling, communication acts, methods for getting attention, attention-getting behavior, and norms for getting attention. Varieties of discourse markers frequently used by Deaf ASL users include tapping on the table or on the floor to get others' attention, and waving an arm and/or hand in the air to get someone's attention.

71. C: Contact signing is designed to help bridge the communication gap between Deaf and hearing people. It is not considered a separate language by linguists. Contact signing is the current name for what was in the past called Pidgin Signed English (PSE). The name was changed in the interest of accuracy because according to linguists, contact signing differs from the usual definition and conventions of typical pidgin languages. Not only is contact signing not a language; it also is never used by signers at home. It is only used to facilitate communication between Deaf and hearing people when either or both do not know the other's language well enough.

72. B: It is correct that Deaf people with formal educations are found to sign using syntax (sentence structure) more similar to English due to their greater exposure to English, while non-educated Deaf people use more non-English, ASL structures in their signing. Though ASL is perceived visually and spatially rather than aurally, it is nonetheless subject to regional dialects. As with English, Northern Americans sign faster and Southerners more slowly, New Yorkers and Californians sign similarly, Texas-Mexico border town residents mix Spanish and American sign languages just as the hearing produce "Spanglish," et cetera. Socioeconomic status is widely perceived in the Deaf community as influencing ASL signing, as are age, race, and gender.

73. C: SEE can mean Signing Exact English or Seeing Essential English. Anecdotal evidence is that historically, many parents were uncomfortable with signing, so school administrators created a title

107

without the word "signing." According to experts, while most of the Deaf community do not know or care about SEE 1 and SEE 2, Deaf Educators tend to use SEE 1 to mean Seeing Essential English and SEE 2 to mean Signing Exact English.

74. A: The SEE signing methods are invented sign systems. They were invented to represent English through the hands. Hence they are not the same as ASL, which does not translate English into manual signs but is a separate language of its own which has developed and evolved rather than being invented. Being invented, the SEE signing methods are not natural systems. They were designed to help Deaf children learn English by showing it visually. Hearing students of ASL should be aware they may encounter these when people use completely different signs.

75. A: SEE 2 is based upon the "2 of 3" rule: The "3" are spelling, pronunciation, and meaning. If two out of these three match across two concepts, the same sign is used for both; if at least two do not match, different signs are used. For example, the English word "wind" as in to wind a watch, a long winding road, or to wind up somewhere, versus as in a wind blowing, has the same spelling in each case, but the pronunciation and meaning are both different. Since 2 of 3 criteria do not match, two different signs are used in SEE 2 for these. The SEE 1 signing method is based mainly upon English syllables rather than the SEE 2 method.

76. B: The Deaf community does have its own distinct culture; however, that culture is also contained within the larger hearing culture, which hence has some influence upon it. Deaf culture is not the same as hearing culture with only minor differences; communication modes alone constitute major differences. Since Deaf culture is a minority contained within the majority hearing culture, it is not unaffected by this. As a minority, Deaf culture does not have a greater influence upon hearing culture than vice versa.

77. C: Most sign language interpreters do two-way work, i.e. they can translate spoken English into signs and can also translate signs into spoken or written English. Some interpreters may be better at reception than expression or vice versa, but they are generally bilingual in sign and English. Signing and interpreting are not interchangeable synonyms. Many Deaf people use signing as their first and/or only language but do not know how to interpret, a skill that requires training. While signing and interpreting do mean different things, it is not correct that they can never be separated. Interpreters can sign, but signers cannot necessarily interpret.

78. D: Many college students who are Deaf and primarily sign to communicate still prefer using real-time captioning stenographers rather than sign language interpreters. This is because interpreters working live make many mistakes, while stenographers can type more precise visual representations of a student's message. While many Deaf have lower reading levels because their language development lacked the benefit of auditory input and feedback, there are also many Deaf Ph.Ds. Many Deaf students who primarily sign have excellent command of English as well.

79. A: Most of your vision should be directed at the signer's face to see facial expressions. You can attend to the other body parts involved with your peripheral vision. Beginning ASL learners will need to focus on the signer's hands at times to see the details of certain signs, but should not constantly focus only on the hands. Especially in real life, eye contact is more important with signers. It is impossible to focus on all three areas at the same time, so the primary focus should be facial.

80. D: In Deaf culture, it is acceptable to walk at normal speed in between signers having a conversation. Standing still or moving very slowly between them might be considered rude, but it is understood in Deaf culture that sometimes people have to walk through a signed conversation.

People are not expected to wait until the conversation ends or pauses. People are not expected to do unnatural things like crouching or taking unnecessary detours. If the person walking maintains a steady, normal pace, the signers can track this and shift a bit to adjust for it momentarily as s/he walks through, such that their conversation is not even interrupted or made slower.

81. B: Ninety percent of children who are Deaf or Hard of Hearing (DHH) have hearing parents. Only 10 percent of hearing loss is caused by congenital conditions inherited from the parents; the rest is caused by environmental or developmental (including heritable but not congenitally apparent) conditions in the child before, during, or after birth. The majority of DHH children do not have Deaf parents, which has implications for education, socialization, and Deaf culture. The proportion is nowhere near half-and-half. It is not true that percentages cannot be measured accurately; the U.S. Census Bureau and various Deaf organizations have done so.

82. C: TDD and TTY are devices that help Deaf people to use telephones. Respectively they stand for Telecommunications Device for the Deaf (TDD) and Teletypewriter (TTY). These are not devices for helping Deaf people to use radios, televisions, or computers.

83. A: TTY stands for Teletypewriter; this term reflects older technology, wherein an electromechanical device used telegraph or telephone wires to transmit message signals. TDD, or Telecommunications Device for the Deaf, reflects newer technology wherein the devices transmitting such signals are electronic. Both have been used for the same purpose: to enable Deaf people to communicate via telephone. Deaf Educators note that many Deaf people still refer to today's TDDs as TTYs out of habit as they have become accustomed to the older term.

84. D: Experts advise that you should remember that you are communicating *with* the Deaf person *through* the interpreter and look mainly at the person you are communicating with as you would in any conversation. You should not "stare" at the Deaf person 100 percent of the time as this would be perceived as "sort of freaky" (Vicars) since the interpreter is another person involved in the interaction. Thus it is expected and more normal to look at the interpreter at times, but mainly to look at and speak directly to the Deaf individual.

85. B: According to Deaf Education experts, when a hearing adult loses his or hearing, s/he does not automatically become a member of the Deaf community by virtue of hearing loss. This person would be considered a member of the Hearing World who now cannot hear. For example, people who are still "hearing" psychologically are depressed/angry about their hearing loss, have not learned ASL, do not have their TV's closed captions turned on, still belong to hearing churches/social clubs, have mostly/all hearing friends, do not subscribe to Deaf publications, have not memorized the number for the relay service (for telephony with no TDD/TTY on at least one end), and wish they could hear again. Joining Deaf culture involves an acculturation process, including reversals of the aforementioned characteristics. There is no "transitional" community. Those becoming Deaf as adults may or may not develop full Deaf identity and Deaf community membership, which will not depend solely on learning ASL.

86. C: Deaf people have historically encountered job discrimination in all of the following ways: They have been hired less. Employed Deaf people have been offered *fewer* opportunities for job-related training. They have had distinctly *less* access to information in the workplace via employers not providing alternate means to access it. They have received fewer opportunities to advance their careers. Deaf employees also have received *fewer/less frequent* promotions to managerial and/or supervisory positions.

87. B: The great majority of culturally Deaf Americans, if it were possible to gain hearing, would refuse such an offer as they do not view hearing as a benefit the way hearing Americans do. The culturally Deaf in America do not consider their "deafhood" to be a disability. Deafness is part of their culture and they value it. They do not view being deaf as a problem needing a solution; they embrace it. They not only accept being deaf; moreover, they think "...it is fine to be Deaf." (Vicars, 2006)

88. D: There are Deaf people in America who subscribe to the clinical/pathological or medical model of deafness, but according to experts, they are most likely not fluent in ASL. They are also not considered "culturally Deaf" as they take a pathological view of deafness and hence are usually not members of the "cultural deaf community." The culturally Deaf take a cultural view of deafness, seeing it as involving culture and language rather than seeing it as a disability as the medical model does.

89. A: Culturally Deaf Americans are known to give much more extensive and detailed biographical and social information about themselves to other culturally Deaf people upon being introduced than the hearing do. They are *more* likely to hug each other in greeting than hearing people. They tend to take *more* time to say good-bye than the hearing. And they usually prefer to socialize around a kitchen table than in a living room, because the lighting is brighter in the kitchen, which is better for the visual communication of ASL. These are all common aspects of Deaf culture.

90. C: According to Audism Free America is correct. "Audism is attitudes and practices based on the assumption that behaving in the ways of those who speak and hear is desired and best. It produces a system of privilege, thus resulting in stigma, bias, discrimination, and prejudice—in overt or covert ways—against Deaf culture, American Sign Language, and Deaf people of all walks of life." Audism has nothing to do with enhancing residual hearing or educating the DHH. It is a bias in favor of the hearing and against the Deaf.

91. A: There is no identification of "informational" audism by experts in Deaf Education or in teaching ASL. Such experts define types of audism as existing at the institutional level, for example, school systems or universities having no accommodations available for DHH students. In addition to the cohesiveness of Deaf culture, the difficult of surmounting audism in such institutions is another reason schools for the Deaf have been popular. Ideological audism exists at the level of philosophies, beliefs, and values. Individual audism exists in any person who is biased against Deaf and toward hearing people and behaviors.

92. B: Linguicism is defined as: "Ideologies and structures which are used to legitimate, effectuate, and reproduce unequal division of power and resources (both material and non-material) between groups which are defined on the basis of language." (Skutnabb-Kangas, 1988) Linguicism describes biased systems producing inequity of linguistic groups. It is not an equal emphasis on the importance of any language, a way of defining social groups by languages, or a philosophy of using linguistics (the study of language) to study cultures.

93. C: Experts in the Deaf community point out that in the "mainstream" hearing population, people have the idea that baldly identifying someone as "Deaf" is rude and politically incorrect. They prefer to make terminology, and reality, softer and less direct by using "hearing-impaired" (as also with "visually impaired," etc.). According to the National Association of the Deaf (NAD), the hearing mean well by this term, but the Deaf resent it and are often offended by it. They dislike its emphasis ("impaired") on what they can*not* do. Taking pride in their Deaf culture, they do not necessarily view deafness as impairment.

94. D: If a hearing person is motivated to learn ASL because of having a Deaf relative(s), s/he should identify them when meeting a Deaf person simply because s/he might know the relative. The Deaf give more background information during introductions because it is highly likely they share common acquaintances due to the smaller size and cohesive identification of the Deaf community. Deaf people recognize they will not share the same commonalities with hearing people, so they do not expect as much background information on meeting them. While there are many thousands of Hearing schools, there are only a few dozen (residential) Schools for the Deaf, so identifying the Deaf school one attended is significant, but Hearing schools need not be identified as the Deaf would be less likely to recognize them.

95. D: The Deaf President Now (DPN) protest in Washington, D.C. in 1988 was a reaction against the trustees' choice of the only hearing candidate out of three finalists to become the seventh President of Gallaudet University. The other two candidates were equally well qualified and were both Deaf. Gallaudet students and other members of the Deaf community protested, resulting in the Hearing candidate's resignation, the Board of Trustees agreeing to Deaf people comprising a 51 percent majority, and the appointment of the first Deaf President of the University. DPN did not involve the office of POTUS, general electoral policies at all American universities, or looking for a Deaf candidate for Gallaudet's President as there were already qualified candidates.

96. C: The Consumer Action Network, founded in 1993, constituted a significant advance for various groups devoted to DHH issues because it formed the first coalition to represent multiple organizations, bringing them together when they had never been unified before. The NAD, founded in 1880, has worked with the United Nations to acknowledge the linguistic rights of Deaf people worldwide to have access to education and information in sign language and to professional sign-language interpreters, and advocates for promoting the national and international cultural and linguistic identity of the Deaf community. The ASDC, founded in 1967, is a national organization to support, inform, and encourage families raising Deaf children. The ASLTA is a national organization devoted to improving and extending the teaching of Deaf Studies and ASL.

97. B: Championing oralism would not be well received by the culturally Deaf in any case and would not make this joke work in ASL. In fact, the giant's final statement does not literally praise oralism, but rather is a use of ironic humor: Deaf culture hates oralism, so the giant's assumption that oralism would have saved the young woman is ironic and hence funny. This joke works in ASL because the dramatization of the giant's, woman's, and townspeople's expressions by the signer can be done perfectly, and is visually active. It works in ASL also because of its linguistic humor: The sign for "MARRY" is produced such that the giant squashes the woman in his palm.

98. A: Title I of the ADA provides that private employers and state and local government employers cannot discriminate against persons with disabilities, which by government definition includes the deaf and hard of hearing. Title II of the ADA provides that state and local governments must make their services, programs, and activities accessible to persons with disabilities, including the deaf and hard of hearing. Title V, Section 504 of the Rehabilitation Act of 1973 provides that any program or activity receiving federal funds, or conducted by any executive agency or the U.S. Postal Service, cannot deny participation in or benefit from such programs/activities to anyone otherwise qualified solely on the grounds of disability. Title V, Section 501 of the Rehabilitation Act of 1973 provides that the federal government must practice affirmative action in hiring and promoting employees with disabilities, including being deaf or hard of hearing, to make reasonable accommodations for them and to give them equal access to opportunities for training and promotion.

How to Overcome Test Anxiety

Just the thought of taking a test is enough to make most people a little nervous. A test is an important event that can have a long-term impact on your future, so it's important to take it seriously and it's natural to feel anxious about performing well. But just because anxiety is normal, that doesn't mean that it's helpful in test taking, or that you should simply accept it as part of your life. Anxiety can have a variety of effects. These effects can be mild, like making you feel slightly nervous, or severe, like blocking your ability to focus or remember even a simple detail.

If you experience test anxiety—whether severe or mild—it's important to know how to beat it. To discover this, first you need to understand what causes test anxiety.

Causes of Test Anxiety

While we often think of anxiety as an uncontrollable emotional state, it can actually be caused by simple, practical things. One of the most common causes of test anxiety is that a person does not feel adequately prepared for their test. This feeling can be the result of many different issues such as poor study habits or lack of organization, but the most common culprit is time management. Starting to study too late, failing to organize your study time to cover all of the material, or being distracted while you study will mean that you're not well prepared for the test. This may lead to cramming the night before, which will cause you to be physically and mentally exhausted for the test. Poor time management also contributes to feelings of stress, fear, and hopelessness as you realize you are not well prepared but don't know what to do about it.

Other times, test anxiety is not related to your preparation for the test but comes from unresolved fear. This may be a past failure on a test, or poor performance on tests in general. It may come from comparing yourself to others who seem to be performing better or from the stress of living up to expectations. Anxiety may be driven by fears of the future—how failure on this test would affect your educational and career goals. These fears are often completely irrational, but they can still negatively impact your test performance.

> ### Review Video: <u>3 Reasons You Have Test Anxiety</u>
> Visit mometrix.com/academy and enter code: 428468

Elements of Test Anxiety

As mentioned earlier, test anxiety is considered to be an emotional state, but it has physical and mental components as well. Sometimes you may not even realize that you are suffering from test anxiety until you notice the physical symptoms. These can include trembling hands, rapid heartbeat, sweating, nausea, and tense muscles. Extreme anxiety may lead to fainting or vomiting. Obviously, any of these symptoms can have a negative impact on testing. It is important to recognize them as soon as they begin to occur so that you can address the problem before it damages your performance.

> **Review Video: 3 Ways to Tell You Have Test Anxiety**
> Visit mometrix.com/academy and enter code: 927847

The mental components of test anxiety include trouble focusing and inability to remember learned information. During a test, your mind is on high alert, which can help you recall information and stay focused for an extended period of time. However, anxiety interferes with your mind's natural processes, causing you to blank out, even on the questions you know well. The strain of testing during anxiety makes it difficult to stay focused, especially on a test that may take several hours. Extreme anxiety can take a huge mental toll, making it difficult not only to recall test information but even to understand the test questions or pull your thoughts together.

> **Review Video: How Test Anxiety Affects Memory**
> Visit mometrix.com/academy and enter code: 609003

Effects of Test Anxiety

Test anxiety is like a disease—if left untreated, it will get progressively worse. Anxiety leads to poor performance, and this reinforces the feelings of fear and failure, which in turn lead to poor performances on subsequent tests. It can grow from a mild nervousness to a crippling condition. If allowed to progress, test anxiety can have a big impact on your schooling, and consequently on your future.

Test anxiety can spread to other parts of your life. Anxiety on tests can become anxiety in any stressful situation, and blanking on a test can turn into panicking in a job situation. But fortunately, you don't have to let anxiety rule your testing and determine your grades. There are a number of relatively simple steps you can take to move past anxiety and function normally on a test and in the rest of life.

> **Review Video: How Test Anxiety Impacts Your Grades**
> Visit mometrix.com/academy and enter code: 939819

Physical Steps for Beating Test Anxiety

While test anxiety is a serious problem, the good news is that it can be overcome. It doesn't have to control your ability to think and remember information. While it may take time, you can begin taking steps today to beat anxiety.

Just as your first hint that you may be struggling with anxiety comes from the physical symptoms, the first step to treating it is also physical. Rest is crucial for having a clear, strong mind. If you are tired, it is much easier to give in to anxiety. But if you establish good sleep habits, your body and mind will be ready to perform optimally, without the strain of exhaustion. Additionally, sleeping well helps you to retain information better, so you're more likely to recall the answers when you see the test questions.

Getting good sleep means more than going to bed on time. It's important to allow your brain time to relax. Take study breaks from time to time so it doesn't get overworked, and don't study right before bed. Take time to rest your mind before trying to rest your body, or you may find it difficult to fall asleep.

Review Video: **The Importance of Sleep for Your Brain**
Visit mometrix.com/academy and enter code: 319338

Along with sleep, other aspects of physical health are important in preparing for a test. Good nutrition is vital for good brain function. Sugary foods and drinks may give a burst of energy but this burst is followed by a crash, both physically and emotionally. Instead, fuel your body with protein and vitamin-rich foods.

Also, drink plenty of water. Dehydration can lead to headaches and exhaustion, especially if your brain is already under stress from the rigors of the test. Particularly if your test is a long one, drink water during the breaks. And if possible, take an energy-boosting snack to eat between sections.

Review Video: **How Diet Can Affect your Mood**
Visit mometrix.com/academy and enter code: 624317

Along with sleep and diet, a third important part of physical health is exercise. Maintaining a steady workout schedule is helpful, but even taking 5-minute study breaks to walk can help get your blood pumping faster and clear your head. Exercise also releases endorphins, which contribute to a positive feeling and can help combat test anxiety.

When you nurture your physical health, you are also contributing to your mental health. If your body is healthy, your mind is much more likely to be healthy as well. So take time to rest, nourish your body with healthy food and water, and get moving as much as possible. Taking these physical steps will make you stronger and more able to take the mental steps necessary to overcome test anxiety.

Mental Steps for Beating Test Anxiety

Working on the mental side of test anxiety can be more challenging, but as with the physical side, there are clear steps you can take to overcome it. As mentioned earlier, test anxiety often stems from lack of preparation, so the obvious solution is to prepare for the test. Effective studying may be the most important weapon you have for beating test anxiety, but you can and should employ several other mental tools to combat fear.

First, boost your confidence by reminding yourself of past success—tests or projects that you aced. If you're putting as much effort into preparing for this test as you did for those, there's no reason you should expect to fail here. Work hard to prepare; then trust your preparation.

Second, surround yourself with encouraging people. It can be helpful to find a study group, but be sure that the people you're around will encourage a positive attitude. If you spend time with others who are anxious or cynical, this will only contribute to your own anxiety. Look for others who are motivated to study hard from a desire to succeed, not from a fear of failure.

Third, reward yourself. A test is physically and mentally tiring, even without anxiety, and it can be helpful to have something to look forward to. Plan an activity following the test, regardless of the outcome, such as going to a movie or getting ice cream.

When you are taking the test, if you find yourself beginning to feel anxious, remind yourself that you know the material. Visualize successfully completing the test. Then take a few deep, relaxing breaths and return to it. Work through the questions carefully but with confidence, knowing that you are capable of succeeding.

Developing a healthy mental approach to test taking will also aid in other areas of life. Test anxiety affects more than just the actual test—it can be damaging to your mental health and even contribute to depression. It's important to beat test anxiety before it becomes a problem for more than testing.

> **Review Video: Test Anxiety and Depression**
> Visit mometrix.com/academy and enter code: 904704

Study Strategy

Being prepared for the test is necessary to combat anxiety, but what does being prepared look like? You may study for hours on end and still not feel prepared. What you need is a strategy for test prep. The next few pages outline our recommended steps to help you plan out and conquer the challenge of preparation.

STEP 1: SCOPE OUT THE TEST

Learn everything you can about the format (multiple choice, essay, etc.) and what will be on the test. Gather any study materials, course outlines, or sample exams that may be available. Not only will this help you to prepare, but knowing what to expect can help to alleviate test anxiety.

STEP 2: MAP OUT THE MATERIAL

Look through the textbook or study guide and make note of how many chapters or sections it has. Then divide these over the time you have. For example, if a book has 15 chapters and you have five days to study, you need to cover three chapters each day. Even better, if you have the time, leave an extra day at the end for overall review after you have gone through the material in depth.

If time is limited, you may need to prioritize the material. Look through it and make note of which sections you think you already have a good grasp on, and which need review. While you are studying, skim quickly through the familiar sections and take more time on the challenging parts. Write out your plan so you don't get lost as you go. Having a written plan also helps you feel more in control of the study, so anxiety is less likely to arise from feeling overwhelmed at the amount to cover.

STEP 3: GATHER YOUR TOOLS

Decide what study method works best for you. Do you prefer to highlight in the book as you study and then go back over the highlighted portions? Or do you type out notes of the important information? Or is it helpful to make flashcards that you can carry with you? Assemble the pens, index cards, highlighters, post-it notes, and any other materials you may need so you won't be distracted by getting up to find things while you study.

If you're having a hard time retaining the information or organizing your notes, experiment with different methods. For example, try color-coding by subject with colored pens, highlighters, or post-it notes. If you learn better by hearing, try recording yourself reading your notes so you can listen while in the car, working out, or simply sitting at your desk. Ask a friend to quiz you from your flashcards, or try teaching someone the material to solidify it in your mind.

STEP 4: CREATE YOUR ENVIRONMENT

It's important to avoid distractions while you study. This includes both the obvious distractions like visitors and the subtle distractions like an uncomfortable chair (or a too-comfortable couch that makes you want to fall asleep). Set up the best study environment possible: good lighting and a comfortable work area. If background music helps you focus, you may want to turn it on, but otherwise keep the room quiet. If you are using a computer to take notes, be sure you don't have any other windows open, especially applications like social media, games, or anything else that could distract you. Silence your phone and turn off notifications. Be sure to keep water close by so you stay hydrated while you study (but avoid unhealthy drinks and snacks).

Also, take into account the best time of day to study. Are you freshest first thing in the morning? Try to set aside some time then to work through the material. Is your mind clearer in the afternoon or evening? Schedule your study session then. Another method is to study at the same time of day that you will take the test, so that your brain gets used to working on the material at that time and will be ready to focus at test time.

STEP 5: STUDY!

Once you have done all the study preparation, it's time to settle into the actual studying. Sit down, take a few moments to settle your mind so you can focus, and begin to follow your study plan. Don't give in to distractions or let yourself procrastinate. This is your time to prepare so you'll be ready to fearlessly approach the test. Make the most of the time and stay focused.

Of course, you don't want to burn out. If you study too long you may find that you're not retaining the information very well. Take regular study breaks. For example, taking five minutes out of every hour to walk briskly, breathing deeply and swinging your arms, can help your mind stay fresh.

As you get to the end of each chapter or section, it's a good idea to do a quick review. Remind yourself of what you learned and work on any difficult parts. When you feel that you've mastered the material, move on to the next part. At the end of your study session, briefly skim through your notes again.

But while review is helpful, cramming last minute is NOT. If at all possible, work ahead so that you won't need to fit all your study into the last day. Cramming overloads your brain with more information than it can process and retain, and your tired mind may struggle to recall even previously learned information when it is overwhelmed with last-minute study. Also, the urgent nature of cramming and the stress placed on your brain contribute to anxiety. You'll be more likely to go to the test feeling unprepared and having trouble thinking clearly.

So don't cram, and don't stay up late before the test, even just to review your notes at a leisurely pace. Your brain needs rest more than it needs to go over the information again. In fact, plan to finish your studies by noon or early afternoon the day before the test. Give your brain the rest of the day to relax or focus on other things, and get a good night's sleep. Then you will be fresh for the test and better able to recall what you've studied.

STEP 6: TAKE A PRACTICE TEST

Many courses offer sample tests, either online or in the study materials. This is an excellent resource to check whether you have mastered the material, as well as to prepare for the test format and environment.

Check the test format ahead of time: the number of questions, the type (multiple choice, free response, etc.), and the time limit. Then create a plan for working through them. For example, if you have 30 minutes to take a 60-question test, your limit is 30 seconds per question. Spend less time on the questions you know well so that you can take more time on the difficult ones.

If you have time to take several practice tests, take the first one open book, with no time limit. Work through the questions at your own pace and make sure you fully understand them. Gradually work up to taking a test under test conditions: sit at a desk with all study materials put away and set a timer. Pace yourself to make sure you finish the test with time to spare and go back to check your answers if you have time.

After each test, check your answers. On the questions you missed, be sure you understand why you missed them. Did you misread the question (tests can use tricky wording)? Did you forget the information? Or was it something you hadn't learned? Go back and study any shaky areas that the practice tests reveal.

Taking these tests not only helps with your grade, but also aids in combating test anxiety. If you're already used to the test conditions, you're less likely to worry about it, and working through tests until you're scoring well gives you a confidence boost. Go through the practice tests until you feel comfortable, and then you can go into the test knowing that you're ready for it.

Test Tips

On test day, you should be confident, knowing that you've prepared well and are ready to answer the questions. But aside from preparation, there are several test day strategies you can employ to maximize your performance.

First, as stated before, get a good night's sleep the night before the test (and for several nights before that, if possible). Go into the test with a fresh, alert mind rather than staying up late to study.

Try not to change too much about your normal routine on the day of the test. It's important to eat a nutritious breakfast, but if you normally don't eat breakfast at all, consider eating just a protein bar. If you're a coffee drinker, go ahead and have your normal coffee. Just make sure you time it so that the caffeine doesn't wear off right in the middle of your test. Avoid sugary beverages, and drink enough water to stay hydrated but not so much that you need a restroom break 10 minutes into the test. If your test isn't first thing in the morning, consider going for a walk or doing a light workout before the test to get your blood flowing.

Allow yourself enough time to get ready, and leave for the test with plenty of time to spare so you won't have the anxiety of scrambling to arrive in time. Another reason to be early is to select a good seat. It's helpful to sit away from doors and windows, which can be distracting. Find a good seat, get out your supplies, and settle your mind before the test begins.

When the test begins, start by going over the instructions carefully, even if you already know what to expect. Make sure you avoid any careless mistakes by following the directions.

Then begin working through the questions, pacing yourself as you've practiced. If you're not sure on an answer, don't spend too much time on it, and don't let it shake your confidence. Either skip it and come back later, or eliminate as many wrong answers as possible and guess among the remaining ones. Don't dwell on these questions as you continue—put them out of your mind and focus on what lies ahead.

Be sure to read all of the answer choices, even if you're sure the first one is the right answer. Sometimes you'll find a better one if you keep reading. But don't second-guess yourself if you do immediately know the answer. Your gut instinct is usually right. Don't let test anxiety rob you of the information you know.

If you have time at the end of the test (and if the test format allows), go back and review your answers. Be cautious about changing any, since your first instinct tends to be correct, but make sure you didn't misread any of the questions or accidentally mark the wrong answer choice. Look over any you skipped and make an educated guess.

At the end, leave the test feeling confident. You've done your best, so don't waste time worrying about your performance or wishing you could change anything. Instead, celebrate the successful completion of this test. And finally, use this test to learn how to deal with anxiety even better next time.

> **Review Video: 5 Tips to Beat Test Anxiety**
> Visit mometrix.com/academy and enter code: 570656

Important Qualification

Not all anxiety is created equal. If your test anxiety is causing major issues in your life beyond the classroom or testing center, or if you are experiencing troubling physical symptoms related to your anxiety, it may be a sign of a serious physiological or psychological condition. If this sounds like your situation, we strongly encourage you to seek professional help.

Thank You

We at Mometrix would like to extend our heartfelt thanks to you, our friend and patron, for allowing us to play a part in your journey. It is a privilege to serve people from all walks of life who are unified in their commitment to building the best future they can for themselves.

The preparation you devote to these important testing milestones may be the most valuable educational opportunity you have for making a real difference in your life. We encourage you to put your heart into it—that feeling of succeeding, overcoming, and yes, conquering will be well worth the hours you've invested.

We want to hear your story, your struggles and your successes, and if you see any opportunities for us to improve our materials so we can help others even more effectively in the future, please share that with us as well. **The team at Mometrix would be absolutely thrilled to hear from you!** So please, send us an email (support@mometrix.com) and let's stay in touch.

> **If you'd like some additional help, check out these other resources we offer for your exam:**
> http://mometrixflashcards.com/TExES

Additional Bonus Material

Due to our efforts to try to keep this book to a manageable length, we've created a link that will give you access to all of your additional bonus material:

mometrix.com/bonus948/texesasl